A Student's Guide to Online Learning

A Student's Guide to Online Learning

Find success in digital study

Gina May and Tim Bentley

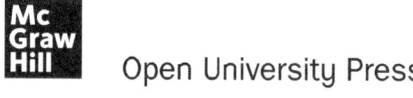
Open University Press

Open University Press
McGraw Hill
Unit 4,
Foundation Park
Roxborough Way
Maidenhead
SL6 3UD

email: emea_uk_ireland@mheducation.com
world wide web: www.openup.co.uk

Copyright © Open International Publishing Limited, 2022

All rights reserved. Except for the quotation of short passages for the purposes of criticism and review, no part of this publication may be reproduced, stored in a retrieval system, or transmitted, in any form or by any means, electronic, mechanical, photocopying, recording or otherwise, without the prior written permission of the publisher or a licence from the Copyright Licensing Agency Limited. Details of such licences (for reprographic reproduction) may be obtained from the Copyright Licensing Agency Ltd of Saffron House, 6–10 Kirby Street, London EC1N 8TS.

A catalogue record of this book is available from the British Library

ISBN-13: 978-0-3352-5162-9
ISBN-10: 0335251625
eISBN: 978-0-3352-5163-6

Library of Congress Cataloging-in-Publication Data
CIP data applied for

Typeset by Transforma Pvt. Ltd., Chennai, India

Fictitious names of companies, products, people, characters and/or data that may be used herein (in case studies or in examples) are not intended to represent any real individual, company, product or event.

Praise page

"A Student's Guide to Online Learning offers a friendly and welcoming introduction to world of online learning. Filled with tips and honest advice, it will help any student choosing this approach to their studies to navigate and succeed in their studies. It is an essential guide for anyone considering online learning – whether wholly online or through blended learning."

Natacha Harding, University of Winchester

"Gina May and Tim Bentley have written a must-read guide for anyone who is considering studying online. The readers are provided with answers to the many questions that students have before and during their studies. The authors act as mentors throughout and supply the right tools to allow the reader to find their confidence and enjoyment in online learning."

Yolanda De Iuliis, Student Support Worker, The Open University, researcher and host of podcast 'Conversations About Mithras'

"This book is an accessible and friendly introduction to online learning, with straightforward steps which build confidence. Chapters on key skills like researching online and maintaining academic integrity encourage students to see themselves as part of a wider research community, tackling the isolation often experienced by distance learners on an academic level. Both new and experienced students will benefit from the clarity the authors bring to the sometimes confusing experience of studying online. Gina and Tim are dependable guides through common areas of worry, ranging from how to start a forum conversation to finding the most suitable assistive technologies. This book is a treasure-trove of ideas, practical tips, and thoroughly sensible advice!"

Dr Cora Beth Fraser, Associate Lecturer and Honorary Research Associate with The Open University

"A Student's Guide to Online Learning is a thoroughly researched, well-written resource which will be useful for those on both sides of the computer screen in the modern academic world, allowing blended and distance learning students to achieve their potential in an online classroom. The material has been well-designed to meet the needs of many groups, including students new to digital study and tutors or lecturers aiming to explore or refresh their understanding of the best ways to reach their online student base."

Ellen Boekee, B.A. (Hons.), M.A.

"This is a comprehensive 'know how to' guide for all things that you need to know about being an online student. There are many exercises that help you work through the various scenarios that may come your way and gives you the tools to make sure that you know how to just about anything. If you are planning to be an online student, I recommend you give this amazing book a read."
Sarah Jones, BA hons Education Studies Primary, Open University Students Association President 2020-2022

"This book is a 'must have' for all students studying any course with an on-line element. Its strength lies in the fact that it covers a very wide range of internet issues, ranging from the very basic to the more advanced. In this book, a student at any level of on-line understanding would be able to find help for potential problems. I do not think there is another book available which has such a wide remit and thus I would recommend this thoroughly to all those studying courses which involve on-line learning."
Gaynor Taylor, Associate lecturer in Classics, The Open University

Contents

1	INTRODUCTION	1
2	ONLINE IDENTITY AND PERSONAS	10
3	LEARNING IN ONLINE ENVIRONMENTS	29
4	ACCESSING LEARNING AND PEER SUPPORT	52
5	RECOGNISING STRENGTHS AND OVERCOMING DIFFICULTIES AND DISABILITIES	66
6	ACADEMIC INTEGRITY AND EMPLOYABILITY	85
7	RESEARCHING ONLINE	98
8	DIGITAL TECHNOLOGIES FOR LEARNING ONLINE	112
9	USING SOCIAL MEDIA FOR LEARNING ONLINE	126
10	TROUBLESHOOTING, STAYING SAFE ONLINE	141

Bibliography *153*
Appendices *157*
Index *164*

1 Introduction

Online learning courses are fast becoming the most popular ways of studying with more and more universities, colleges and professional trainers offering a wide range of options. These include blended learning courses which have part of the teaching online and part face-to-face; courses which are delivered completely online with or without tutor guidance and free options such as Massive Online Open Courses (MOOCs). All of these come under the terms remote, online, blended or distance learning.

These terms, particularly the 'distance learning' and 'remote' elements, could be seen as a negative because they seem to imply that students are left on their own to study, with no contact with other learners or support from tutors. So, if you have just signed up for a course like this or been asked to do one as part of your professional development, you may be feeling a little apprehensive. But there are lots of different ways of interacting with others when learning online. Once you get the hang of these, the 'distance' disappears and learning online can become a positive experience because it means that you can fit your study around work, family, friends and life events.

How is online learning different?

Learning online is different from going into class each week where you meet your tutors and fellow learners face-to-face. In standard face-to-face courses, you know what the other students on the course look and sound like. The atmosphere will probably be fairly relaxed, and the group might chat before and after the class and make contributions to discussions during the sessions. When we are talking to others in a face-to-face situation, it is not just words that make up the conversation. It is often the tone of voice, facial expressions and body language that say as much as the words themselves. They all contribute to the meaning of what we say and, importantly, how others hear it.

When learning online, probably most of the communication you have with your tutor and fellow students will be in writing, whether in emails, forums, chatrooms or whatever other kind of interface that your institution uses. This may seem strange at first, but you will soon get used to it, and may even come to prefer it. However, communicating only in the written word can sometimes be tricky as the words that you write, or read, are open to misinterpretation. Strategies for how to manage this are provided in Chapter 2, *Online Identity and Personas*.

Blended courses have both face-to-face and online elements to them. Part of your time will be spent on campus in lectures or seminars while others will be delivered only online. Some learning institutions record and even live stream their lectures and seminars, which means that you have a choice of either attending in person or remotely from another location.

The good thing about the online elements of blended and distance learning courses is that you do not have to take time travelling to a classroom. Instead, the classroom is with you all the time: in your laptop, tablet or maybe even your phone. You can study at your own pace in your own time and fit it around your everyday life. The only designated times that you may have to be physically present in an online learning room would be for tutorials. These will probably also be recorded, so if you do miss them for any reason, you will still be able to catch up. You will not have to carry lots of course books around or find a place at home to store them.

The whole campus, and all of your study material, will be online and neatly tucked away in your laptop, tablet or phone. There is a whole range of digital technologies that help make learning online enjoyable. These are discussed in Chapter 8, *Digital Technologies for Learning Online*.

Choosing a course that is either blended or entirely online

Choosing a course where part, or perhaps all, of the teaching and learning is done online may be your only option depending on what is being offered by the university or college you have chosen to study with, or because of your personal circumstances.

When you are attending online classes as part of a blended learning course, or studying a course that is taught entirely online, it can feel as if you are isolated and working completely alone, in a kind of bubble. You may feel that you are the only one who is worrying about a particular part of the course, or perhaps you just want someone to talk to about the ideas that you have.

Whether you have chosen to study remotely, or it is something that you have no choice about, you may be apprehensive about how it will all work in practice and what will be expected of you. But you will not be the only one in your cohort who is worried, and you have made a good start by reading this book!

Come back to this activity later once you have started the course and have had time to settle into it. See if your answers have changed, or if you rank them in a different order. Once you get to know other people on the same course, you will probably find that they have similar reasons.

There will almost certainly be a welcome forum before the course begins where you can introduce yourself and get to know a little about your fellow students. Why you decided to study the topic and why you chose to study online might be something that you can start a conversation about in the forum where everyone can join in.

You will all have an interest in the subject you are studying and so there will always be something to talk about if you are not comfortable talking about

> **Activity 1.1**
>
> Think back to when you first decided to sign up for an online or blended learning course. It may be that you have thought about it for a long time, or perhaps it was a snap decision. What were your reasons for wanting to do the course? If you have not yet signed up, why are you considering doing a course with some or all its elements online, and what might the advantages be? Rank them here in order of importance.
>
> 1.
> 2.
> 3.
> 4.
> 5.

yourself. Once you get started, sharing ideas, hints and tips with others is also a good way of using the forum space.

I consider myself to be disabled – will I be able to manage?

The major course providers are very experienced in making course materials accessible to everyone, whether or not they consider themselves to be disabled. For those who are unable to travel, or to travel alone, online courses are a great choice as it means that it is possible to participate as fully as everyone else on the course without leaving home.

Those who have additional requirements, learning difficulties or other, hidden, disabilities may need extra time for submitting assignments or for doing exams, and most course providers put in place tailored solutions. This may include offering extensions of the due date for assignments to allow you more time to work on them, extra time in examinations and even the option of taking exams at home with a visiting invigilator.

Printed and bound copies of the online-only course materials are usually available on request and if you contact the Student Support Team of the course provider, they will be able to suggest other ways that they can help you (see Chapter 3, *Learning in Online Environments,* for the practical issues of being an online learner and Chapter 5, *Recognising Strengths and Overcoming Difficulties and Disabilities*).

The important thing is to get in touch with your college or university in advance of the start date if possible so that everything you need can be put in place before the course begins. If you are in the UK, you may also be eligible for the Disabled Students' Allowance, so it is worth checking the gov.uk website for more details about eligibility and how to apply. More on this in Appendix 3.

How will I access the course material?

All courses, including blended and distance learning courses, will offer you a Student Home Page and it is there that you will find everything you will need. You may be sent hard copy course books, but for most online and blended learning courses, instead of having books arrive in the post, they will be in a digital format available at the click of a mouse on your Student Home Page. These can be downloaded in a variety of different formats for you to use on your desktop, laptop, tablet or phone. Any set books that you need to buy will either be in hard copy or in a digital format so, if there is a choice, you can decide which you prefer. There will also be a study planner telling you what you should be doing each week.

Even though you may be very used to reading for pleasure, reading for 'learning' is different and you are likely to cover unfamiliar, possibly very difficult, material. Whether you are using digital or hard copy formats, you might want to highlight sections or put notes in the margin as you go along. Once you have the 'books', and if you decide to work with the digital versions on- or offline, you will also be able to bookmark them so that you do not lose your place as you read.

There will also be links to other areas of the course website that contain information about getting help with study skills and academic writing, accessing the library, joining the forums, attending the learning events, a portal for uploading assignments and much more. It is worth finding out if you can send a dummy assignment at some point before the first one is due to make sure that the format you will be using is compatible with your course leader's marking software.

Is online learning right for me?

One of the major advantages of online courses is that they are designed for a wide range of abilities. Most, if not all, education-based courses have basic study skills built into them. This might mean learning an entirely new set of skills, or it might be a refresher depending on what stage of education you are at. This is because the providers recognise that a lot of the people who choose to study online have diverse reasons for doing so and one of these may well be the lack of previous opportunity to study in a conventional way.

Whether the things covered in the study skills sections of the course are something you can already do or not, it is still useful to go over them. You will either learn something new or find out that you are doing it correctly. Either way, it is a good use of your time.

Activity 1.2

Write down three study skills that you feel confident about and three you might need to learn or brush up on.

Things you feel confident about	Things you need to learn or brush up on
1.	1.
2.	2.
3.	3.

If you have already enrolled, locate the areas on the Student Home Page where you can access study skills help and details of the format and referencing style used by your chosen institution.

Will I fit in?

You may feel worried that you will not be able to keep up because other people on your course know much more than you. This is unlikely to be the case and people learning online, as well as at brick colleges and universities, are usually very supportive of each other, no matter what educational background they might come from.

Actually, people in an online learning space tend to be more supportive of their peers than on most face-to-face courses because everyone is aware of the particular difficulties of studying online. Most people are keen to establish and maintain some kind of contact with others on their course precisely because they are so far apart. Sometimes it is just a case of taking the plunge!

Once you have joined a course, got started and joined in with some of the conversations in the forums, or even just read them, you will soon see that there are many other people in the same situation and with the same educational background as you.

Take a look at the student comments below:

I left school at 15 without any qualifications, that was twenty years ago! I never liked school much but now I really want to catch up on what I missed. I've been doing an access course which will get me ready to go to university, and if I pass it, no, when I pass it, I'll do the degree online too. No one in my family has ever been to university so I will be the first. I can't wait to get that bit of paper! (Dionne, Monkton)

I started my degree studying online last year. At first I was really worried about not finding the time with all the other things that I had to do, but it has worked out ok. I am getting reasonable grades and I am really proud of myself. I am beginning to feel like a proper student! (Dan, Broadstairs)

I had planned to go to a brick university after my A levels, but I was worried about getting into massive debt with a student loan. In the end, I decided to do my degree online not just because it is quite a bit cheaper, but I can carry on working as well which really helps. I wasn't sure what to expect but it's turned out to be ok. When people ask me what I do, I say 'I'm a student', and I tell them that I am working at the shop to pay my living expenses. (Megan, Margate)

I wanted to get back to studying but with two babies it was near impossible for me to get childcare either during the day or in the evenings if I was going to do a part-time course. Not only that, but paying a babysitter was not an option I could afford. Being able to study online has made it possible for me to start working towards getting a degree, which will mean I can eventually apply for teacher training when the children go to school. It has also given me back my confidence and I feel like my old self again. (Samantha, Birchington)

As you can see, there is no particular 'type' of person who studies online, or who goes back into education after a break, long or short. No matter whether you have just finished school or college, or you are going back into education after a gap, it is only natural to be apprehensive when starting to learn again, whether that is online or not. But remember, there will always be people who feel just the same as you.

Establishing common ground

Getting involved in all aspects of your course is important and can be very rewarding. But if you do not necessarily like crowds, or social gatherings, while you will probably need to contribute to online activities that form part of the course, you do not need to get involved in the more social discussions if you do not want to. There are lots of different ways of interacting with other people in an academic environment. Once you get started, the 'distance' disappears and learning online and attending lectures and seminars remotely, or through recordings, becomes a real bonus.

If your course has a welcome forum where you can meet your fellow students before the course begins, it is a good idea to join in if you can. If you are not comfortable contributing to the chats, log on anyway and read what other people are saying. That way, when the course gets underway and you start working in the online forums, or attend welcome functions, you will already know some of the others in your group and this will make you feel much more comfortable.

If your course does not have a welcome forum, it will almost certainly have a Facebook page set up either by the course provider or by former or current students, so it is worth having a look for it and joining. If there is not already one in existence, you could think about setting one up yourself and acting as its moderator.

When you do join in, you will to need to think about how you want to be perceived by the tutor and others on your course and think about building your online academic identity (see Chapter 2, *Online Identity and Personas* for more on this). The most successful and enjoyable online learning comes when there is a continual exchange of ideas between the tutor and students, and between the students themselves.

How should I talk to the others on my course?

Meeting the other people on your course will be very different from a face-to-face classroom situation because you cannot see what the others look like unless people upload a photo. The only thing you will have is the written word. Therefore, communicating can be tricky and it is important to consider the way in which your words might be received by others in the group. This is something that will be covered in Chapter 2, *Online Identity and Personas* and Chapter 6, *Academic Integrity and Employability*.

What do people say about studying online?

Learning remotely is not for everyone because it is such a different way of doing things. People are used to being physically present with other people for some, if not all, of the day. But during and following the global COVID pandemic of 2020, people were alone or in household groups for extended periods of time. This saw a major change in the way that people communicated and learned. With schools, colleges and universities closed, the learning and teaching *had* to be done online. This meant that using technology as a way to study and stay closer to others, albeit virtually, became even more important, and more sophisticated, than ever before.

The outcome has been that many course providers decided to keep in place the online or blended learning strategies that they had devised.

For universities and colleges who had always delivered their courses online, the original teaching and learning strategies remained unchanged. However, the pandemic prompted an increase in research studies which looked at the particular difficulties faced by remote learners, such as feelings of isolation giving way to stress. It was noted that these issues were directly connected to the progression and retention of students.

Here is what some students said about learning online:

Positive experiences studying online

> I have done lots of online courses. Once I had done one, I was hooked. I really like the way that I can study at home, in the park or even on the train on my way to work. I quite like studying by myself as I don't feel like I am letting anyone down if I have to do a bit less one week and catch up on it the next. (Sally, Margate)

> I have all the information I need in my tablet. The books, the course material, even the tutor and the other students in a way! I can watch the recordings of any tutorials I have missed, stopping and starting them if I want to make notes or look something up. I can also read what the other students have said on the forum and join in with that if I want to. (Ellen, Carlisle)

> If the course had not have been online there is no way that I could have done it. To be honest, I was worried at first that I might not be able to manage doing it all on my own but I soon became familiar with the technology and found it ok in the end. (Sheila, Manchester)

Negative experiences studying online

> I didn't realise when I signed up that I wouldn't get any books. I find it really hard to concentrate for very long looking at the computer, so in the end I printed all of the material so I could read it on paper. (Rosemary, Kent)

> The thing that I find really hard is being on my own. I like being around people, so not being able to see the people I am talking to in an actual classroom is a pity. (Marjorie, Herne Bay)

> This is the first time that I have ever studied online. I struggled a bit with the technology side of it and couldn't get into the online classroom for the first couple of weeks. I managed it in the end though with the help of the computer help desk. (Harriet, Whitley Bay)

While it might take a bit of getting used to, studying online is a different, but convenient, way of learning either for pleasure or for a qualification (see Chapter 3, *Learning in Online Environments*). With lives getting ever busier, being able to study at your own time, in your own space, is often the thing that makes the difference between whether or not to sign up for a course.

There are now thousands of blended and online courses available, covering just about every topic imaginable, which means that finding the right course for you has never been easier.

Summary

All the topics talked about above, and lots more, are covered in the various chapters of this book so that you can approach, study and complete any blended or online course that you undertake with confidence. The main thing is to start early so that you are familiar with where everything on the course website is before the course begins, so that you can concentrate on the learning and not have to worry about the technicalities or the technology.

2 Online Identity and Personas

By the end of this chapter you will be able to:

- create an online profile
- start threads in an online forum
- communicate appropriately with your tutor
- word online posts appropriately
- communicate effectively with your peers
- understand the concept of netiquette.

Creating an online profile

You probably already have an online identity, on Facebook, LinkedIn, Instagram, Twitter or some other platform. You may even have more than one social network profile, each of which may say different things about you depending on what they are and who you are communicating with.

You might have an account with a supermarket if you do your shopping online. Maybe you use online book sellers or auction sites. You will also have some kind of online profile if you have a mobile phone or an internet connection.

For each one of your online profiles, you will have a username and password so that you can access your account and the online services provided. These profiles make up part of what is called your 'digital footprint'. This is where you have been, and what you have looked at, said or done online.

The profile and persona which you create in an academic online space may be different again and in keeping with your other online accounts, you will be able to control what information it holds and what it says about you.

You may find that you have more online profiles than you realised. Or perhaps you did not consider an account as an online shopper as being part of your profile. But each one of those holds information about you such as your name and address, and probably your date of birth. Similar information will be required by the provider of an online course, but in keeping with the others, your information will be kept secure under the General Data Protection Regulations (GDPR). Further help with keeping your information secure can be found in Chapter 10, *Troubleshooting, Staying Safe Online*.

As with most other online services, when you sign up to an online course, probably one of the first things you will be asked to do is to create your profile

Activity 2.1

Make a list of all the different social media profiles that you have. Include things like Facebook, Twitter, Instagram, etc. Then write down the different username(s) that you have for each one. (Do not write your passwords in this book, remember to keep these secure at all times.) Finally, write down what your username is on other platforms such as shopping, social contact, reading the news, etc.

Platform	Username	Platform	Username
e.g. Facebook			
e.g. Twitter			
e.g. Instagram			
e.g. Internet			

and upload a photo. The only part of this that will be seen by other students in your class is your username and image. The other details such as your address, date of birth, etc. will be held securely in accordance with the GDPR in keeping with your other online profiles.

Creating a profile for an online course is very much like creating a profile in any kind of social media such as Facebook, Instagram or in a more work-centred platform like LinkedIn. The difference is that the information you put on your profile, and the kind of things that you might discuss in the forums, will be less personal and more academic in nature. For instance, you may want to create a profile that talks about why you have chosen the course, what you hope to get from it, your research interests, or things that you would like to study in the future.

Activity 2.2

What are the five things that would showcase you professionally? Rank them in order of importance (with 1 being the most important and 5 being the least).

1.
2.
3.
4.
5.

What are the five things about you as a person that you think are most interesting? Rank them in order of importance (with 1 being the most important and 5 being the least).

1.
2.
3.
4.
5.

What are five things about yourself that you think are suitable to talk about in an academic or professional forum? Rank them in order of importance (with 1 being the most important and 5 being the least).

1.
2.
3.
4.
5.

When creating your profile in an educational space such as that provided by a college, university, work-based or private course provider, your username is the name that appears on the site and on any related forums. This should be your real name. This is important because it allows the person teaching the course to see who is contributing to the discussions. They can also step in to answer questions and offer help or guidance about any forum or group work that is being done and, if necessary, contact you direct.

These types of forums will be 'closed', which means that only the tutor and the other people who are doing your course will be able to see what is posted. You will be given a link and a password to the main site and your Student Home Page before the start of the course so that you can access everything you need to know.

When you have signed into the site, it is a good idea to change your password to one that you will be able to remember easily. It is not a good idea to use the same password across multiple sites or to allow your computer to automatically save them for you.

Once you have done this, you will probably be asked to upload a photograph. It is always best to do this if you can because it is one of the quickest and easiest ways to take the 'distance' out of distance learning. It means that the group of people on the course are not talking into a void as this makes effective communication difficult. Being able to see each other's faces, even if it is only in a photograph, helps to create a connection.

This connection is very important because it helps form a bond with the other people on the course, which in turn makes it easier to have academic discussions and do group work because it all feels more comfortable and familiar. It helps you make the transition from the real world to the virtual world and back again. It will also make you more confident in the space generally because it will feel less anonymous.

Being able to see who you are talking to makes a huge difference to the confidence and trust that is built up in the group as a whole because it will feel as if you know one another, even if only in a small way, and this will make it easier to ask questions about the course materials or assignments. When you are studying online, on your own at home, it is very easy to feel isolated. But there will certainly be other people feeling the same way so anything at all that you can do individually, or as a group, will help to bring down these barriers. Uploading a photo is a very good start.

If you do not want to put up a photo of yourself, you could consider using an avatar that is related in some way to your profession, a picture of a pet or even a cartoon character that you think resembles or represents you in some way. Before the age of photography and online communication, the personality, position and power of a person was also demonstrated through an image.

Even the ancient Romans made a statement about who they were by placing a portrait on one side of a coin and an image of one of the gods, or from myth, on the other. This sent out a powerful statement to everyone across the Roman Empire about how they saw themselves and how they wanted others to see them.

Activity 2.3

Have a look at the photographs you have of yourself either on your phone, computer or in print. Do you have anything that you think is suitable to upload as your profile picture? If not, why not try taking a few 'selfies' and see how they come out. Decide which one you will use as your profile picture.

What do you see behind you and what does it say about your life? Then look at the clothes that you are wearing. What might they say about you as a person?	
Go onto Google Images and look at the photographs of people in general and see if you can tell what sort of person they are, or what you can learn about them from the background of the image.	
Now find a photo of you that is how you might want a prospective employer, tutor or fellow student to see you.	

The thing to remember when you are choosing what to put up as your profile image, is that a learning space is visible to people with whom you may well develop an academic or professional relationship which moves from the online space into the real world.

The online persona

The online persona is different from a digital footprint because the footprint shows which online sites you have visited, which pages you have looked at, what you have bought, etc. The 'persona' is the aspect of ourselves that we show to others and how they perceive us. It is similar to an actor who takes on a particular role. In our real lives, we may act or even speak a little differently in various circumstances, such as when we are at work or with our friends, but we are still the same person. 'Being' on the internet is different because it is largely anonymous, and people will only get to know you 'as a person' from what you choose to tell them in particular circumstances.

This also applies in an online learning situation where it is very likely that you do not know the other people on the course. It may be tempting to reinvent yourself, perhaps as someone who knows more about the topic than you really do, or to make yourself sound more interesting. But it is much better to just be yourself.

The online space that you occupy as part of your course is a 'workspace'. Imagine that your job meant that you worked from home some, or all, of the time. In this kind of situation, you would have to apply the principles laid down by your employer for that workspace and you would interact online in the same way that you would when face-to-face in the physical workspace. Studying online should be the same.

Have a look at the comments below from students talking about how they feel about their academic online persona:

> *I'm not very good with people and online I feel more like myself. No, I mean more like the self I wish I was.* (Louise, Lincoln)

> *Online I don't have to be me. I make out that I know more than I really do by going onto other sites and finding things, and sometimes copying out of a book making out that I said it. No one knows where I got it from so it looks like I'm really clever.* (Robert, Middlesbrough)

> *I built this whole profile of myself with a good job and loads of qualifications. But then when someone on the course told me about a job at their firm that I really was qualified to do, I couldn't even go to the interview. I was worried that everyone would find out that I had been lying. I wish I had just been honest in the first place because I missed out on what would have been a really good move for me.* (Michael, Sevenoaks)

Creating an online persona does not have to mean pretending to be someone or something you are not. It is like writing your CV, where of course you showcase yourself in the best possible light, and when appropriate, demonstrate your talents and your achievements, but it is important to be honest.

Being in an online learning situation is not the same as social media where some people might exaggerate and pretend that their lives are more exciting and glamourous than they really are. Professionalism and authenticity are key to maintaining a credible academic or professional online presence, but this needs careful and continual management.

Honesty and integrity

It is very easy to find out information about people via the web, so it is important to maintain an honest online persona no matter what type of digital space you are in. It only takes a few clicks of the mouse on a mainstream search engine such as Google or Bing to find out where people live, what jobs they have had and the kind of things they buy on auction sites like eBay. And because you may have a presence on a number of online platforms, it is inevitable that at some point, they will overlap.

Just because the online learning space is not an open forum, it does not mean that it can be a place for escapism or role play. It is part of the online campus provided by the governing institution and what happens online, stays online, *permanently*. Whatever you say or do will leave behind a digital footprint even long after it has been deleted.

Welcome forums

The Welcome Forum is likely to be the first time that you will 'meet' your tutor and fellow students. This is the same as if you were attending a face-to-face class for the first time. You would probably choose something suitable to wear, be on time and greet the others in the group when you arrived. If the tutor asked people in the room to introduce themselves, you would do so. Maybe from the beginning, or at least at some point, you would join in with the discussions and make a contribution to any group work that was set.

Doing the same thing for an online course is, of course, a little different, but the two do have things in common. The forum is just like having a conversation, but it is asynchronous (not in real time), so you may have to wait for a response to what you have said. This delay has its advantages because when you come to answering what someone else has said, you have time to consider their post and think about what you want to say in your response.

Your tutor will probably post a welcome message, and then it will be the turn of the tutor group members to join in and introduce themselves. First impressions count. It is good to be friendly, but always bear in mind that this is an academic rather than a social space. Some suggestions are your name, the area where you live, what you do for a living and why you are studying the course.

Have a look at the thread below:

Norma (moderator): *Welcome to this Tutor Group Forum. I'm Norma, your tutor. This space is a closed forum where you will be able to interact only with me and your fellow tutor group students. I will use this as a teaching space where you will take part in online tasks, and I will also be posting discussion threads throughout the year. But before that, let's use this thread to introduce ourselves and say a little bit about who and where you are and why you are studying the course. Over to you!*
John: *Hello Everyone. My name is John and I live in Yorkshire. I retired two years ago and since then have been catching up with all the studying I missed when I was younger. I love literature and I'm really looking forward to learning about the Victorian period.*

Caroline: *Hello Norma and John. I'm Caroline. This is my second attempt at this course because just before the end of last year I became ill and with a toddler to look after as well, I had to defer. But I am back now and determined to succeed! I'm much more comfortable online than face-to-face so studying like this is perfect for me. I live in London.*

Lizzie: *I'm Lizzie, from Kent. Me too Caroline! I can't get to face-to-face events but the forums and Facebook pages are an amazing support – they also offer us a great sense of belonging. I'm excited to get started on the course and look forward to getting to know you all!*

You could start a conversation yourself by creating your own thread and talking about something to do with the course that is likely to attract the interest of others. Posts of more than about five lines tend not to be read, which means that they often go unanswered and this can be disheartening and knock your confidence. But it is not because what you have said is not interesting, it is just that it is too long, and people may not have the time to read it all the way through. Keeping posts short means that they are more likely to elicit a response and get the discussion going.

It is best to avoid talking about yourself too much as this would probably be seen as pushy or 'loud' and might remain unanswered, not for any other reason than it would be difficult to think of something in response. This is an easy mistake to make when you do not know anyone and feel as if you have nothing in common. However, what you *do* have in common is the course that you are studying and so it is always a safe bet to talk about that. Ending on a question makes room for other people to come into the thread as they can answer you.

Activity 2.4

Have a go at drafting your welcome post in the box below to include your name, where you live, something interesting about yourself and why you are studying the course. Ideally, the post should be no more than five lines long.

Netiquette

Online learning requires respect and collegiality from everyone in the group. The term 'netiquette' is short for 'internet etiquette' and is a code that governs polite behaviour online. There is no official 'legal' definition of the term but when signing up for an online course, you will be asked to confirm that you are willing to follow the guidelines set down by the institution. These are likely to include the following rules:

1 Be respectful of other forum users' feelings and do not post inflammatory, bullying or belittling comments on the work of others, or on their posts.
2 Respect the privacy of your fellow students and do not share any personal information, posts or images.
3 Do not use offensive language either as a direct comment or as part of an anecdote or joke.
4 When replying to posts, respond to those that came before so that they are not ignored.
5 Stick to the topic when posting in threads.
6 If someone asks a question and you know the answer, offer to help while being respectful.
7 Do not SHOUT in posts. Using upper-case letters is equivalent to shouting in normal speech.
8 Be mindful of your tone of voice and be friendly and supportive at all times.
9 Before starting a new discussion, check that the same point has not already been brought up. If it has, reply to the existing thread rather than start your own.
10 If you see any breach of the netiquette rules, please contact the moderator.

The forum moderator will keep an eye on the forum and joint working spaces to make sure that the netiquette rules laid down are adhered to.

Keyboard bravery

This is the phrase for the phenomenon where people write things online that they would not ordinarily say if they were face-to-face with another person. Another phrase you might hear is 'keyboard warrior'. This is an unpleasant way of behaving that sets out to dominate a conversation, intimidate others and disagree with what is being said in a forceful or offensive tone.

Sometimes people do not realise the way their words might affect others and that the written word does not contain any verbal cues that might soften the tone, or even give the words another meaning altogether.

It is the responsibility of everyone to consider carefully what they say and if you are posting something which might be seen as controversial, or emotive, it is better to draft the post, but not upload it until the next day. Then you can check in with what you have said before putting it up on the forum to make sure that its content and tone are suitable for the task. Remember that the people you are studying with do not know you and so the only thing they have to judge you by is the way you behave. Your 'behaviour' is the things that you say and how you say them, in the forums.

Unfortunately, sometimes when lots of different characters come together, someone dominates the conversation by being 'loud'. This means making long posts which leave no room for anyone else to come into the discussion. Or perhaps answering posts in what feels like a superior tone, which makes others feel intimidated and, as a result, unwilling to add anything to the thread in case they are criticised in some way.

Conversely, the person who appears to be dominating the conversation may themselves be worried about posting and in order not to miss anything out, writes long posts and long replies. If you break down what is being said, you may see that a lot of the points made are in fact relevant but that there are just a lot of words surrounding it.

Have a look at what these students say about writing on forums:

> *Getting to talk about the texts was the best part of the course as far as I was concerned. I was the first one to start a thread and I wrote about the things that I had noticed and how I thought this was connected with the module material. I spent ages writing it up and putting in all the references but no one answered it. So I put up another post with more ideas hoping that there would be a response but I was out of luck there too. In the end I just said that if no one else is bothered then why should I be? It was ridiculous!* (Elaine, Glasgow)

> *I was quite nervous about going on the forum because obviously I didn't know anyone and I'm normally the last to speak up anyway. Right from the beginning there was this man who wrote really long posts and he sounded really smart. I was scared that if I said something about the paintings we were studying, he would say that it was wrong. So in the end, I didn't say anything.* (Nola, Poole)

In the quotes from students above, you can see two different points of view. The first is from a student who is very enthusiastic and wants to talk about what she is learning. However, she did not realise that by saying too much, she was intimidating other students who were less confident. This can be seen from what the second student says about her experience.

Sometimes there are others in the group who respond with equally long posts, and between them the two parties dominate the learning space. It is the responsibility of the moderator to manage this and to make sure that there is enough room for everyone to take part in the online discussions. It is not a good idea to get involved in any kind of conflict by confronting them. The moderator will have almost certainly have seen this happen before and will know how to resolve it.

If you notice any breach of netiquette, or behaviour that could be offensive or belittling to yourself or other forum users, it is best not to confront the person yourself as this may set off a chain of unpleasantness. Instead, contact the moderator of the forum (usually your tutor) without delay. They will have the tools and the authority to remove the offending post and speak to the person involved.

What you could do, however, if you feel comfortable to do so, is take a more subtle and friendly approach. Have a look at the forum thread below:

Title: Online learning task 1 (20% of the overall module mark): Using your set book, answer the question below.

Norma (moderator): *This is the first of your online tasks. The group discussion question is: How does Dickens involve the reader in the lives of his characters?*
I would like you to think about the way in which the author shows the characters in the book as living in the uncertainty of the time. Also think about how the author creates suspense. Please remember to read the other posts in the thread before replying so that there is a continuous conversation rather than a group of monologues.

John: *It seems to me that the author has created the characters in a really subtle way so that as the action progresses, they mirror the plot. The first part introduces the reader to what it was like living in the Victorian period. This makes the reader experience the ups and downs of characters' lives. I've read lots of books like this. The hero and the heroine both come from different social backgrounds. Well they think they do, which is why things get so complicated towards the end. John*

John: *Well, it looks like no one else is going to say anything so I might as well say a bit more. I was surprised by the amount of descriptions of places in the book. It meant that I could recognise them and from that figure out exactly where it is that he was talking about. I think this makes the suspense more real because I can imagine the people in their own homes. The symbolism that he uses is very dark as well and so this adds a lot of suspense.*

When a person seems to know so much, the forums can be fairly quiet apart from their voice. In a situation like this, you could say something along the lines of the response below.

Lara: *Hello Norma and John. What an interesting question Norma. John, you seem very knowledgeable about the book so I don't know what else I can add really. Come on group, Norma said she doesn't want a group of monologues so let's really get behind this question! John has made a good start, so now we can pick up the discussion and carry on from there. Thanks John! I've been thinking about how colour might be important. What do others think?*

To 'make space' for yourself to join in the discussion, if someone appears dominant, imagine that you are in a classroom and the discussion is happening in real time. Going over and over the written word can make us read so much more into the intention of the writer. It might have come across very differently if you were all talking face-to-face because you would have less time to think about it and nuance would be added to the words by the tone of voice and facial expression of the speaker.

In ordinary circumstances, you might choose to remain a 'lurker', that is someone who reads and learns from the forums but does not actively contribute. If you are more comfortable with doing this, that is fine. In the same way as listening to others as they talk, a lot can be learned from reading a discussion as it develops, allowing it to inform your own thinking, helping you to decide what you think about a topic. But in a situation where it is a credit bearing exercise, you would need to find some way of being able to carry out the task. If you are at all worried, speak to your tutor, as there may be an alternative task you can do.

One way to break the cycle of a monologue is to respond with a question in a light-hearted way as shown in the example above and encourage the rest of the group to get involved. The important thing is to *respond*, and not *react*, taking time to think about what you are going to say and making sure that your own post does not seem to be belittling or bullying in any way.

Activity 2.5

Have a go at drafting a post in response to the two entries by John, above. How would you stay within the rules of netiquette by acknowledging his posts before going on to write your own?

Activity 2.6

Now try writing a response to Lara's post in a way that responds to what she has said, being sure to make room for others to join in.

Once someone posts a response and opens up the space again, more people will feel confident to get involved. But if you do not feel comfortable with posting a response, do not give up on the forums, just drop your tutor an email. They will take steps to make sure that everyone feels at ease in the learning space and is able to contribute in a meaningful way.

Email communication with your tutor or course leader

As well as communicating in the forums, you will probably have most of the contact with your tutor via email. It will start with a welcome email from them either at or shortly before the start of the course. As with forum communication, first impressions can only be made once. Take a look at the sample email below and the two responses. Remember that the contact comes from a 'real person', and so normal rules of manners apply. It is important to respond because you would not ignore them if they spoke to you face-to-face in the classroom! It is also important to write the response in the right way.

Tutor: *Welcome to the course! I am looking forward to working with you over the next nine months. The teaching will all take place online and there will be five 'face-to-face' synchronous tutorials together with several asynchronous discussion threads which run alongside them. All the details of when and how these take place are on your Student Home Page together with the links you will need to access them. I would be grateful if you could reply to this email so that I know you have received it and that I have all the correct contact details for you. Could you also please say something about yourself, why you have chosen to study this course and what you hope to get out of it. I look forward to working with you. Sincerely, Norma*

Response 1: *Hi Norma – thnx for the email. I want to be a teacher. Cheers, M.*

Response 2: *Dear Norma, Thank you for your email. I am looking forward to getting started on the course and getting to know you and my fellow students. I am taking this course because I want to be an English teacher, so would really like to know more about how to approach and analyse texts. I enjoy reading literature from the Victorian period and I'm especially excited about Unit Two and learning more about the time the books were written in and how this influenced the writers. I have checked the contact details on my home page and they are all correct. Thank you again for your email, Best wishes, Megan*

Response 1 is too colloquial and although technically it answers the question, it could be seen as abrupt and impolite. Text speak should be reserved for texts and should never be used in emails or academic forums as there is a risk that it may not be understood. Using the right 'voice' for the type of contact you are having is a very important part of establishing your online identity. Every time you 'speak' online you are not just saying *something*, you are also saying something about yourself.

Response 2 is much better and follows the usual conventions of letter writing. It starts with a greeting and an acknowledgement of the initial communication. It then goes on to say something very brief about the writer, explains why they are doing the course and what they want to get out of it. It then ends with a formal sign off. It gives the impression of someone who is articulate, polite and who is committed to studying with a real interest in the material. It also sets up the beginning of that all-important working relationship between the tutor and the student.

Writing an email has the same rules as writing a letter. Unless you are writing to a friend or family member, it should begin with a greeting such as 'Dear Daniel'. It should be clearly articulated and end with a salutation such as 'Yours sincerely' or 'Best wishes'. It should not contain slang or 'text speak' or be over-familiar in tone.

> **Activity 2.7**
>
> Draft a response to the tutor's letter in the box below. Remember that it should have a salutation, acknowledgement, information then formal send off.

Think about the identity that you want to project and how you can start to build a good working relationship. There is no need to make the email overly long; in fact, the more concise it is, the better. The tutor will probably have a lot of students so receiving a long email from each of them would be very time-consuming to read. It is only really necessary to introduce yourself briefly before answering their questions and letting them know anything relevant that might affect your studies such as disability, or anything else that might impact your studies such as shift work or caring responsibilities.

If you text your tutor, it is best to start by introducing yourself and say which course you are taking. This is because your tutor may be teaching more than one course and is unlikely to have the contact details of all the students logged in their phone.

As well as university and career progression courses, there are other ways of learning online. For the most part, when it comes to creating your 'persona', the same rules described above apply, and for the same reasons.

Developing an academic voice

Depending on what you are studying, and the reason you are studying it, there may be a certain style of interacting, or a particular set of vocabulary that is expected. But in any case, the best bet is to remain professional, concise and clear at all times because your words will be memorialised forever once they have been posted.

> **Activity 2.8**
>
> Below is an example of academic voice. Try rewriting the other two phrases, more concisely, using a similar tone of voice. Once you have done this, have a look at Appendix 1 for some suggestions.
>
> | Day-to-day voice | Academic voice |
> | --- | --- |
> | Thanks for that. I was going to have a bit of a rummage later and try and find out where it is. Any clue where the homework is? | Many thanks. I will have a look later to see if I can find it. Do you know how to access the assignments? |
> | Not only is Elizabeth I the largest aspect of the painting, even out of proportion to the surrounding characters and furniture, this portrayal of her really signifies how she is a larger than life character to look up to and makes her this focal point both within this painting but also within Elizabethan society. | |
> | The translation of this letter by Cicero isn't that clear – in the translation he's actually mentioned as one of the speakers, writing was what he did for a living so it's important to him for the speaker – to be known. But in this translation we don't know if he is the actual speaker or not. | |

Quite often in academic forums, there is only a limited time from when the post has been shared to when it can no longer be edited or deleted by whoever uploaded it. After that it will only be the forum moderator who can take it down. Therefore, it is best to get it right first time if you can.

The academic voice you use should be semi-formal in the group discussion areas but formal in any written or assessed work that you submit. The academic voice is one that uses the particular terminology relevant to the academic discipline and topic together with the conventions of the online medium. For instance, if you were having a discussion in a synchronous, real-time format such as Skype or Microsoft Teams, to a certain extent, you would be able to pick up the inference of what was being said from the facial expression and tone of voice of the speaker through your webcam.

It is much easier to have a conversation acknowledging the speaker through your facial expression, which would demonstrate that you were listening to what they said. Nodding as you listen also encourages the speaker and gives them confidence in what they are saying and the same would apply when you were speaking and others were listening to you.

However, when the same conversation takes place in an asynchronous situation such as a forum, you need to consider carefully everything that had already been said in the previous posts in that particular thread before you joined in. This is so that you know what was being talked about, so as not to miss or repeat anything.

If there were a lot of posts and you did not have time to read them all, you could simply acknowledge this by saying something like 'I'm sorry to be coming to this discussion late, I work shifts [or whatever the reason is] and this is the first chance I have had to join in. My apologies if I repeat something that has already been said'. This way you are acknowledging the other speaker(s) and doing what you would normally do in real life should you arrive late at a meeting, which is to apologise and try to catch up on what has happened so far.

Wherever possible, it is also preferable to mention people by name. This is an important part of using the appropriate language, phrased in the right way so as not to cause any offence. Whether you are doing a Continuing Professional Development (CPD) course for your existing job, training in a new job or studying in order to get the qualifications to apply for a job, the specific language you use and the 'tone of voice' in which you say it is very important.

Activity 2.9

What sort of words or phrases are commonly used in your job, hobbies or academic discipline? You will be surprised how many different types of vocabulary you use. List them here and give an alternative that others outside of that 'discourse community' would understand.

Specialist word	Meaning
e.g. A bobber (fishing)	A float
e.g. Badger (cricket)	An enthusiastic player
e.g. Methodology (essay writing)	The way in which it will be approached

Making sure that you are using the right vocabulary and tone is also important when you are creating an online presence that a prospective or current employer might look at. Do a quick search of your name in Google and Google Images now and see what comes up. Do the same in other platforms you use or have used in the past. Do you like what you see?

If there is there anything, even from years ago, that you would not particularly want your current or prospective employers to see, you can request that it be taken down. If it is on your own Facebook page, either remove it or change your privacy settings. Twitter posts can be deleted.

MOOCs

MOOCs are Massive Open Online Courses which are usually free and, as the name suggests, open to anyone. If you are joining a MOOC, you will need to register using your name, email address and sometimes other details. This is so that the moderators who are responsible for keeping an eye on the comments can get in touch with you if they need to. However, as this is such an open space, you are able to create your own username, which need not necessarily be your real name, and it is this that will be outward facing. You can choose anything you want to as long as that username is not already being used. You might use initials from your first name and surname, for example, Emily Dyett might become ED80 from the initials plus house number, or perhaps Myett.

There are often thousands, maybe even tens of thousands, of people from across the world taking part in a MOOC at any one time. Because of this, the moderators of the course will not make personal contact with you but nevertheless, it is still important to project the right persona.

Continuing Professional Development courses

If you are doing a CPD course, you should compile a profile that outlines your position and role in the workplace. In a space such as this, it is important to think very carefully about how you present yourself and what you say about your experience. Your online self will invariably spill over into the real world and so it would be unwise to exaggerate any qualifications or experience you might have.

Particular care should also be taken when choosing a photograph to upload. If you work in an industry that requires you to wear a uniform, it is best to upload a photograph of you wearing it. If not, the photograph should show you as professional, wearing smart clothing with nothing in the background. It should be recent and of a high resolution so that it does not blur once uploaded.

In keeping with other online courses there will probably be an introductory thread, so once you have created your profile, the next step is to go into the forum space and have a look to see what the instructor has said. You will also be able to see any messages that have already been posted. This will give you an idea of what kind of wording to use yourself. A typical kind of post might be:

Caleb: *Hello Everybody. I'm Caleb Purland, a regional manager at PP Island Technical. I'm doing this course to find out more about overseas marketing as we are expanding into the global market next year. I'm looking forward to being able to link up with other people who have experience in this field.*

Using the first person and including details of why you are doing the course makes you sound much more approachable, which will be encouraging for those who may be less confident or less used to this kind of learning. As this type of forum is work related, it may be appropriate to either attach your CV or provide links to your workplace profile, or to your LinkedIn page.

But be aware that your professional and personal online profiles may well overlap. It is fine for a potential employer to see your accomplishments in several places, but not so good if they stumble across your profile on social media which has photographs showing you being irresponsible or reckless in your private life.

Summary

Your online identity is made up of facts about you. A variety of companies will also hold personal data about you such as where you live, your job, your date of birth and, in some cases, your bank details, medical records and other information.

This is different to your 'persona', which is much more in your own control and should be treated with caution and reviewed at regular intervals. In an online learning space, you will be connecting with people that you do not know in the beginning and the only things they know about you will be what you tell them. As we have seen above, this includes the photograph you upload, what you say about yourself and how you say it.

Key points from this chapter

- Uploading a photograph to your online learning profile helps to break down the distance in distance learning.
- Other than to close friends and family, emails should always start and end with a salutation.
- Written words can easily be misinterpreted, so they should be chosen with care.

- Getting involved in the online learning forums as soon as possible greatly enhances what you can get out of a course.
- Beware of abbreviations or acronyms because there is a risk of them being misunderstood or considered impolite and inappropriate.

3 Learning in Online Environments

In this chapter you will learn about:

- the practical issues of being an online learner
- developing and maintaining confidence
- how blended courses work
- learning from online activities
- cooperating with tutors and fellow learners
- how to navigate group work tasks.

Is online study right for me?

Many people say that they feel a little apprehensive about starting a new course, whether that is face-to-face or online. But for others, learning online has advantages:

> *For me, the scariest thing is that because I have been out of education for a long time that everybody is going to be younger than me and they will know more. I know that I will have to write essays but I don't think I remember how!* (Dorothy, Canterbury)

> *I am fine with doing a distance learning course because I'm not very comfortable around people and I don't like being put on the spot. Doing the course online means that I can just read the forums and get with learning by myself. I can watch the recorded tutorials back and stop and start them whenever I want, taking notes at my own pace.* (Dan, Broadstairs)

> *This is perfect for me. I don't have a lot of spare time because I work full time and have two children. So most of my studying is going to have to be when they are asleep or in my lunch hour at work. I've already downloaded all the reading so I'm getting a bit ahead with that before the course gets going.* (Louise, Ipswich)

It is easy to imagine that everyone else is more confident and cleverer than you but this is seldom the case. The majority of the group will be just as nervous as you in the beginning.

One of the things that can make you feel more confident is to get to know as much as you can about the course in advance and do any pre-course exercises

Activity 3.1

If you have just signed up for a course, or are considering it, check that you have found out the following information. Make a note of anything else that you need to find out and where you will be able to find the answers.

Query	Answer or where to find out
How to log into the site	
Start date of course	
Student login details	
Titles of any set books	
Types of assignments	
Due dates of assignments	
Contact details of tutor	
Dates and times of tutorials	
Name of the course FB page	

or reading that is suggested. Getting to grips with the technology is also an important part of your preparation so that when the course starts you are able to concentrate on the content and not worry about getting connected or how to use the online tools provided.

Becoming an online student

Before the course starts, there is likely to be a welcome forum, or some other kind of pre-course activities taking place. These are definitely worth getting involved in because you will be able to ask questions about what you will be learning and find out if there is anything that you need to do in preparation. This might be things such as buying set books or brushing up on your study skills. It also gives you the opportunity to become familiar with the course web page and how to use it.

Make sure you have a good internet connection and look at all the resources offered by the university, whether that is the library services or the resources tab for your specific module. Prepare yourself mentally to study alone and understand that you are solely responsible for studying and progressing with your module.

Being part of the learning community is important whether you are studying face-to-face or online. It is where people with the same kind of academic interests come together. As a group, it is also likely that some of you will have the same questions as the course progresses. This is why a group forum is so useful. It allows the sharing of ideas and creates a safe communal place where questions can be asked with the answers being visible to help everyone.

There are a number of other things that you can do to become part of the cohort, such as finding out if there is a Facebook or other social media space, perhaps an area of the main course web page where you can meet past or present students, or perhaps a Students Union page. Joining in is a good idea because it helps you find out more about the course from people have already done it and get in touch with people who are starting at the same time as you.

Being an online student may be different to studying at a brick university in that the learning and teaching takes place via the internet, but it also has some fundamental similarities. The online tutorials that take place in real time (synchronous) are rather like lectures or tutorials.

The forum tasks and discussion points (asynchronous) are similar to seminars where there is a wider discussion with the other students on your course. You will have access to an online library with librarians to help if you cannot find what you are looking for, and there will be course material you need to read and understand followed by assignments with specific submission dates. The tutors or course leaders will be available at certain times, and you will be able to chat to other students informally via the forums or social media.

The virtual campus

One of the main advantages of studying online is that the campus is 'virtual'. It will probably still exist in a brick form and somewhere there will be offices for each discipline, where academics write the course material and assignment questions, and where exam departments work. There will also be IT departments which deal with the uploading of the course material and where all the administration takes place. But unless you are doing a PhD, it is unlikely that you will ever visit it.

For you, the campus is wherever you are. The teaching and learning materials are usually available at the click of a mouse at any time, day or night. You do not even always have to be connected to the internet to study because most of the course materials can be downloaded onto a laptop, tablet or phone. You will not need to spend time travelling to or from a classroom, worrying about parking or childcare and you can create your own timetable for studying. Everything is conveniently accessible in one place.

When you sign up to a course, you will be given all the information you need to log into the course website and from there, you will be able to click through to other services such as the Student Support Team and the library. It is worth spending some time getting to know the site so that you take full advantage of what it can offer you.

> **Activity 3.2**
>
> Make a note of some of the things offered on your Student Home Page and on other pages connected to your course. How might they be useful to you?
>
> | Name of web page | Usefulness |
> |---|---|
> | | |
> | | |
> | | |
> | | |
> | | |

Studying online

Studying a distance learning course is a great way to be able to take part in courses that might otherwise be unavailable to you because of distance or time restrictions. Whether you are studying for a particular qualification, as part of your ongoing skillset for work or just for pleasure, it is only natural to be apprehensive at the beginning.

Getting to know as much as you can about the course and online learning in general will help combat this. You have made a good start by reading this book! Working on your own does not have to be isolating because there will always be opportunities to converse with the tutor and other students on the course, you just need to take part in as much as you can.

On the other hand, it may be that you have chosen an online course precisely because you would rather not meet people face-to-face, speak to people on the phone or take part in forum discussions or group work. If this is the case, it is a good idea to let your tutor know because they will be able to email or text instead of calling you and they may be able to provide you with an alternative assignment to any group work element.

Should you want to, it is possible to just listen in to online tutorials or watch the recordings afterwards. You can also learn from the forums as an objective observer by reading the discussions as they develop.

> *I was fine with writing in the forums and watching the recordings of the learning events but when it came to doing group work online I got really anxious. The thing that worried me most was that I did not know anyone and they all seemed to know more than me. I had a chat with my tutor who calmed me down a bit and persuaded me to have a go, and in the end I got to enjoy it and was proud of the end result.* (Marshall, Edinburgh)

Learning online is, of course, different from going into class each week where you would meet your fellow learners face-to-face. You would know what they looked like and perhaps learn a little about their lives, maybe even become friends. The atmosphere would probably be fairly relaxed and the group might chat before and after the class. Most people would make contributions to discussions during the session.

While studying online means that this does not happen, a very similar atmosphere of collegiality can be created if people join in with the activities and online learning opportunities offered. This may feel a little strange at first if you are not used to talking to people on a video link in one of the online platforms such as Skype or Zoom. But you will not be the only one who is apprehensive, so it is worth persevering because once one person joins in, others probably will too.

Your brain is a muscle

When you first start studying at college or university, you may find that reading, or listening to, course materials makes you tired quite quickly. This is only natural because you are asking your brain to perform a new function that it may not be used to.

Doing any type of course is like training to be an athlete. Your brain is a muscle and when you start to learn new material, in new ways, and to interact with new people, you are using it in a specific way, one related to academia and more specifically to the learning outcomes of your course. The more you use your brain, the stronger it becomes.

This is why it can be useful to begin each learning session with a short task, looking over what you will be reading or working on, perhaps looking at the slides in advance of an online teaching event, or looking over your notes.

Like an athlete, you will be warmed up and it will be easier for you to learn. From there, building in breaks will make sure that you do not do too much in one go. Taking regular breaks and coming away from the screen or other study materials is important. There is no set amount of time that people should study before taking a break because everyone is different, but it is usually recommended that you take a short break each hour.

There are apps that you can download onto your phone or tablet that allow you to input how often you want to take a break and how long for. This means that you do not have to keep checking the time and can concentrate better while you are working. Alternatively, you could set an alarm on your phone or watch to let you know when it is time to take a break. Then, when you have completed what you want to do, you should 'warm down'. This might involve getting things ready for the next online learning event, or downloading, bookmarking and storing what you intend to work on next.

Study space

For an online course, the core material will be online and as such contained within your laptop, tablet or phone, but invariably you will also use other, physical, things. Some courses have hard copy module materials and set books that you need to read and make use of for your assignments, or you may be required to create a portfolio of some kind. Therefore, you will need to find space to store these in your home and set up a study space where you can take part in the tutorials, do your reading, take notes and work on your assignments.

Ideally, you will be able to allocate a particular space in your home where you can set up a desk with all the things you need such as notebooks, pens, course books and printer. It does not matter if this is the end of the dining room table or a corner of a room as long as it is your designated study space and somewhere comfortable with enough room for you to study.

> **Activity 3.3**
>
> Make a list of all the things that you will need to start studying. If there are things that you do not have yet, add where you will get them from. For instance:
>
> | Items you need to get started | Where to get the items from |
> |---|---|
> | Notebooks | |
> | Memory sticks | |
> | | |
> | | |
> | | |
> | | |

Using a particular workspace each time you sit down to study helps you to concentrate and work in a more focused way. Doing this makes the space become almost part of the course itself and when you are in it, you will go into 'work mode'. Courses usually have a recommended number of average study hours per week, which might seem quite high but it is probably an average figure and you might spend less time in some weeks when you are just reading perhaps, and more in others when you are planning and writing an assignment.

You can also create specific study times in your planner for when you will be in the learning space, work out how long you will study for and what breaks you will take. So while having the entire campus on your electronic device is extremely useful because of its portability, this does not mean that the 'old-fashioned' sitting at a desk style learning should be abandoned for studying in a variety of other spaces.

Choosing a comfortable work-spot

For courses that are delivered either partially or wholly online, the physical space that you will work in is very likely to be your own home, and so you will be able to choose where you want to study, whether that is in your own home or somewhere else.

If you decide to study at home, and if you have enough room, you should set up a designated space to study. You will need a desk big enough to hold a desktop or laptop and room for all, if any, additional machinery that you will be using, such as a printer and room for your books, DVDs or CDs and a comfortable chair. This is particularly important if you are using assistive technologies.

If you do not have this space at home, you could consider going to the study area of a local library or university library if there is one near you. They will each usually have a reference area where you can use a table as a study desk.

Local libraries usually have free internet that you can log into and printers that you can use for a small fee per page.

Your workspace should not only contain all the things you need to study, but it should also put you in the right frame of mind for learning.

Your physical environment

Not all learners learn in the same way. Some are visual learners and require a clear workspace devoid of colour and distraction in order to focus on their work. Some are aural learners and require a quiet workspace to help them focus. Others cannot focus unless they have background noise, or music playing. While for others, an array of objects and colour help to stimulate their thought. The important thing is to work out what works best for you.

Activity 3.4

If you are studying at home, think about where you are going to work and the distractions that you might face.

Where will I work?	
What distractions might I face?	
How will I minimise distractions?	

Wherever you choose to study, your physical environment should be comfortable because you are going to be spending a significant amount of time there. If you are away from home, it should have ready access to refreshments and a bathroom. Wherever you decide to study, remember to take regular breaks. Frequent short breaks each hour are recommended as these are more effective than longer breaks every few hours.

Your physical environment should support your study methods. If you make written or printed notes, you will need somewhere to store them, and have some kind of organisational system, so that you can find what you want without having to flick through all your papers.

You will need enough space to base your computer whether it is a desktop, laptop or tower. You will also need enough room for your course books, notebooks, stationery and mouse mat. Your physical environment should also be secure. Your learning is too valuable to leave unlocked and to risk losing it.

Set-up Tip – When you set up your workspace (e.g. at home), take a before and after photo so you can be sure you have achieved what you set out to.

It does not matter if you do not have a permanent place to study at home. Your Personal Learning Environment (PLE) does not have to be fixed, it can be fluid in structure and location so you can study almost anywhere, for instance in a library, a coffee shop or just somewhere quiet. The important things are to be able to concentrate, that there is a secure internet connection and that you can access the resources you need.

Activity 3.5

When you are not at home, think about where else you could study and fill out the table below for each location.

Where I will work? – e.g. in a café.	
What distractions might I face? – e.g. noise from other customers, phone.	
How will I reduce, remove them? – e.g. use earplugs or headphones.	

Use this format and write down any other potential study locations such as on the bus/train, at a friend's house, in the library, etc. Each space has relevance to how effective your Personal Learning Environment will be in augmenting your learning.

Activity 3.6

You have reviewed studying at home and in other locations. What are the main differences between working at home and elsewhere? On balance, where do you think you will be most productive and why?

Location 1:	
Location 2:	
Location 3:	
Location 4:	

Health and safety when studying online

Because most, if not all, of your course material will be delivered online, you will probably spend a lot of time looking at the screen. Whether you are sitting at a desk or table to do this or in some other location, there is a risk of digital eye strain and backache. Ideally, the screen should be directly in front of you and an arm's length.

Try to avoid any glare from windows behind you or from overhead lights. It is also recommended that you use the 20-20-20 method, which means that every 20 minutes you should look away from the screen at something 20 feet away for 20 seconds (Nall, 2018). If your eyes become dry, use eye drops or an eye mist (if you are on any medication, check with your doctor or pharmacist first).

Work in this way to maintain good posture

1. Ensure the top of the screen is level with your eyes, about an arm's length away.
2. Relax your shoulders – try to position yourself high enough so you do not need to shrug your shoulders.
3. Place the computer and screen directly in front of you on the desk or other surface.
4. Have the keyboard just below elbow height.
5. Ensure the back of the seat provides good lower back support (or use a cushion to provide additional back support).
6. The seat height should equally support the front and back of the thighs (or use a cushion to raise the seated position).

7 Have a gap of 2–3 cm between the front of seat bottom and back of knee.
8 Keep the screen and keyboard central – do not twist your back.
9 Have the mouse in line with your elbow.

The height of your chair should allow your arms to form an L shape with 10–15 cm of your forearms resting on the table in front of your keyboard to avoid repetitive strain injury. The chair should support your lower back and your feet should be flat on the floor or supported on a footstool. Frequent breaks will help to avoid muscle pain (NHS, 2021).

If you are reading on a tablet, avoid bending your neck down too far to see the screen as this can cause shoulder and back pain. If you intend to read from it for any length of time, it is a good idea to put it on a stand at a desk or table and adjust your posture (as above) as if working at a computer screen. Frequent breaks should also be taken to rest both your back and your eyes.

Time management

For many people, online learning is a convenient way to obtain new skills while for others learning is an enjoyable hobby. Whatever your reasons for doing a course, it can be difficult finding enough time during the week to carry out the reading, preparation and assignments. A part-time online course usually entails doing 16 hours of study per week.

It might seem sometimes that there is not enough reading or preparation to take up this much time, but the stated study hours will include such things as taking notes, preparing for online tutorials, writing assignments and either doing set forum tasks or taking part in forum discussions. Do not worry, the time will soon be eaten up.

There will be deadlines that you have to meet for the submission of assignments and the details will be in the course handbook or be available on your Student Home Page on the course website. It is your responsibility to stick to these and you will not be prompted by the tutor.

Therefore, as well as storing this information in your phone, computer or hand-written diary, making a paper calendar and putting it somewhere prominent is very useful.

> *The best tip I can give is to look over your module materials before the module begins and plan your weeks of study before even attempting to start. Write down all the activities you need to do for each week of studying and then add your personal circumstances and what other commitments you have. Try to make a realistic timetable to fit in everything so that you don't get stressed over it.* (Andrew, Hertfordshire)

Weekly, monthly and even yearly calendars are available to download from within most word processing packages. Or you might prefer to buy a wall planner.

> **Activity 3.7**
>
> Using the weekly planner below, start by marking with a 'x' all the times that you WILL NOT be able to spend studying, making sure to include employment, household tasks, childcare, travel, shopping, time with loved ones, cooking, eating, bathing, etc. Also mark times that fall before you would normally get up, or after you would normally have gone to bed.
>
> | | MON | TUES | WED | THURS | FRI | SAT | SUN |
> |----------|-----|------|-----|-------|-----|-----|-----|
> | 6–7am | | | | | | | |
> | 7–8am | | | | | | | |
> | 8–9am | | | | | | | |
> | 9–10am | | | | | | | |
> | 10–11am | | | | | | | |
> | 11–12am | | | | | | | |
> | 12–1pm | | | | | | | |
> | 1–2pm | | | | | | | |
> | 2–3pm | | | | | | | |
> | 3–4pm | | | | | | | |
> | 4–5pm | | | | | | | |
> | 5–6pm | | | | | | | |
> | 6–7pm | | | | | | | |
> | 7–8pm | | | | | | | |
> | 9–10pm | | | | | | | |
> | 10–11pm | | | | | | | |

Either way, the main thing is to plot out the key dates of your course and other important life events so that you can find a way to fit everything in.

If you live with other people, putting the calendar where they can see it will help them to support you by making allowances at crucial stages of the course such as when assignments are due.

Remember to put in all the things that you have to do so that you are not caught out by missing the dates on which assignments are due, or when key online learning tasks need to be completed.

Essentially, doing an online course like this is equivalent to taking on a part-time job. So if you treat it as such, you will be able to make the most of your study time.

Finding the best place, time and method of studying is as important as listening to your body clock. For instance, you might be an early riser and be at your best very first thing in the morning, or you may be a night owl who studies better at night. You should plan your study week accordingly.

The gaps that you have left are where you can allocate time to study. You may find that you have plenty of time where you can timetable work related to your course or perhaps you find that you have worryingly very little time to spare.

Using a planner like this means that whether or not you have plenty of time, or very little time, you can make sure that no time is wasted because you can plan in advance and allocate specific things to do in that time such as reading, research or essay writing.

Knowing exactly what you plan to do will mean that none of your precious time is wasted in making those decisions and you can get on with what you need to do straight away. You can grab bits of time here and there in between study times to gather your resources, or bookmark things that you need to read.

Not all your study time will be spent reading or writing. You may also find that some of your time needs to be spent *thinking*. That is, thinking about the content of the material you are learning, giving yourself time to digest it and consider its fullest meaning. This does not need to be done sitting at a computer.

For instance, you can do this while walking the dog, doing the gardening, etc. Whatever you have read and taken notes on will be filed away in your brain somewhere, with your mind making sense of it. We may be resting, but our minds are still working. That is why we sometimes wake up in the night with a brilliant idea!

Keeping a notebook close by to jot down anything that springs to mind can be useful in making sure that you do not lose any of those valuable thoughts. Some of your marks may come from discussions with fellow students, so jotting down your ideas as they come to you means that you will usually have plenty of things to talk about when it comes to group discussions in tutorials or in forum-based exercises.

Using the forum

The forum is a place for you to have almost any kind of discussion (within reason and the rules of netiquette). Not everything has to be to do with course work, it is also a place where you can just 'chat' with your fellow students. This is a very good way of taking some of the distance out of distance learning. It is worth getting involved as soon as you can because it gives you the chance to talk to people with the same interests as you and with whom you will be learning for the duration of the course, and perhaps beyond. Someone has to break the ice and get the ball rolling. Have a look at the forum posts below for how this might look.

Emily: *Hello fellow students! Well, I thought I would get the forum started, I'm a bit nervous but here goes! I've been reading the introduction and it talks about how many essays we've got to write. I thought there was going to be more homework so I'm quite relieved. How about you?*

Megan: *Hi Emily. I know what you mean. It's all new to me and it is taking me ages to get to grips with everything we have to do. But I'm excited to get started.*

Note that Emily's post ends with a question, so this meant that Megan had something to join in with and to talk about in her post. Megan does not end with a question, but between the two posts, there are lots of things that you could pick up on and join in the conversation that way. It might be easier to imagine the conversation taking place face-to-face and think about what you would say if the three of you were sitting having a cup of coffee.

The forum is also a useful place to ask any questions you have about the module or assignments. Unless you are doing a specific group work task, there will almost certainly be rules around collaborative working, so it is not a good idea to mention the specifics of what you are writing in your assignments.

But if, for instance, you have a general question relating to an assignment, the forum is probably the best place to ask it. In this way, you will be helping others on your course who probably have the same question but were afraid to ask! This kind of post immediately makes the group bond. For example:

Emily: *Hi Everyone. I know that this is a silly question but can anyone tell me where the upload button is to submit the essay?*

Megan: *Phew! Not a silly question at all Emily! I thought I was the only one who couldn't find it.* ☺

Lenny: *I know what you mean. It took me ages to find it! It is on the top left-hand side of the Student Home Page under the Resources drop down menu.*

Here you can see that once one person asks the question, others also admit that they have been wondering the same thing. Once one person takes the first step, others will follow.

There will often be online tasks associated with your course material. It might say something like:

> In what way do you think that the source illustrates the idea of authority? Put your answer on the forum in the thread headed Exercise 1 together with two questions that you would like to ask the author. Read the comments of your fellow students and respond to at least three. This task is worth 20% of the overall mark for the course and should be completed by the end of Week 21.

Collaborative learning like this is one of the ways in which online and blended learning courses compensate for not having the kind of face-to-face discussions that you might have at a brick university. It is a way of getting you to articulate your ideas and respond to the ideas of others to create an academic dialogue. This is because when you are studying alone, it is not always easy to recognise the most important points or to develop an understanding of the key concepts of what you are working on.

Not all of the online exercises will be credit bearing, but it is still advisable to do them so that you get the most out of the course. It also helps to expand the way in which you might apply those concepts to other areas. Course materials often suggest various things that would make a good discussion, so these are a useful prompt to help you think of things to post.

If you do not feel confident enough to put your ideas up on the forum or to take part in the online discussions, you should speak to your tutor who will be able to advise and reassure you. Your confidence can be boosted by drafting what you want to say and underlining or highlighting the important parts. In this way, you can double check that you are staying relevant.

Attending tutorials

The actual online teaching element of a course will probably happen in a number of different ways. Some will be via the course materials that you have to read and think about, while others might be done through group discussions or tasks in a forum. These examples are asynchronous learning, in other words not in real time.

But there will also probably be 'face-to-face', synchronous, online tutorials via whichever platform your course provider uses. In these, you will be taught in real time by your tutor and will be able to interact with your fellow students. If at all possible, you should attend as many as you can so as not to miss any vital piece of information that your tutor gives out about the content of the course, or about the assignments.

Having the tutorials and lectures online means that you can take part from anywhere there is an internet signal whether that is sitting at home at the dining room table, or on a beach on holiday. This is called synchronous learning because it happens in real time with the tutor leading the session and you will have the chance to join in any discussions and ask questions. Most learning events are recorded, so even if you did miss one for any reason, you could watch it back at a time that suits you.

Tutorials are a vital part of any course because they might be the only opportunity that you have to speak in real time to others in the group. The dates and times of all the tutorials will probably be given to you once the course starts in a letter or email, or they may be on a tab on your Student Home Page.

You can decide whether or not you put your webcam on for these classes, but if you have a camera on your computer, it is a good idea to use it. If others do the same, you will get to know each other better and this will help make you feel more comfortable when talking or working together in the forums. There will probably be a function that allows you to have a still photograph of yourself in place of a live webcam stream if you would prefer not to have the camera on.

Communicating effectively in writing

The majority of the contact you have with your tutor and fellow learners is likely to be in writing. This will be via email, forum discussions and perhaps some kind of social media. The problem with this is that you will not know each other well and the communication is only via the written word, with no facial expression or intonation to help you interpret the meaning of what people are saying. The same applies to the way in which other people interpret what *you* say.

The meaning of words does not only come from the person who writes them, but to a large extent from the way another person reads them. In some circumstances, the way in which we 'receive' the words can be influenced by what type of person we are, for instance being either a very confident or a naturally anxious person.

> I think I have come a long way since starting this module, and reflecting back on this assignment I feel as though my learning is clicking into place. I think I have done well by being more confident about writing what I think. For example in the group forums in the past, I was more concerned about writing the wrong thing and everyone thinking I was stupid. In this forum however, I realised that everyone learns at their own pace and it's not a problem if we have different answers as every answer is still valid. (Stephen, Newcastle)

Punctuation is also an important part of communicating in writing. It adds meaning to the words, and to a certain extent, implies tone of voice. For instance, when exclamation marks are included, the words can sound as if they are being said quickly and in either an enthusiastic or forceful way. Putting words in capitals implies that you are SHOUTING!

Activity 3.8

Think about your experience of talking (in writing) to other people, friends, family, colleagues or even strangers. Has there ever been a time when there have been misunderstandings? If so, how were these resolved? Did you do anything different after that to make sure it did not happen again, such as using words or punctuation in a different way?

On their own, words are static and so how we put them together and add punctuation creates the meaning we want to get across. But this does not necessarily mean that the reader sees them in the same way as the writer.

The way in which students communicate online has a major impact not only on the enjoyment they get from a course but also the end result in terms of marks. One of the main elements of this is getting to know other students and becoming part of the 'learning community'. Therefore, the way in which the written word is used and received can have an influence on students' final grades.

Because it can be difficult to imagine the way in which people we do not know might interpret what we write, it is a good idea to write the post in draft and not send it straight away. Leave it for a while, or even overnight, and then have another look at it.

Leaving time between writing and posting means that you can look at the words in a more objective way and help to see how the reader might react. This will all become easier and you will become more confident as you go along.

Activity 3.9

Look at the posts below and comment on what sort of person you think each writer is and how you might respond to a post like this if you were doing a group exercise.

Forum post	Analysis
(a) I think it's about time we got on with the task! We haven't even decided which book we are going to talk about!	
(b) Hi Emily, Lenny and Lee, nice to meet you! I'm really looking forward to working with you. I was thinking that maybe we could start the task this weekend if that works for everyone? In the meantime, shall we have a think about which book to use and maybe have a chat about it here on the forum during the week? I was thinking we could do the Gaskell text. What do others think?	

Activity 3.10

Draft a forum post in which you are trying to encourage others to make a start on a group activity. Come back to it later in the day, or after you have finished reading this book, then try to look at it objectively and see what it says about you, and how others might receive your words.

Forum post	Analysis

Contact with your tutor

The tutor is a very important part of your learning when doing any kind of course. Many blended and online courses rely on teaching via online classroom platforms such as Blackboard, Adobe Connect or Zoom. So while you may not have the opportunity to meet your tutor in real life, you will get the chance to meet and talk to them in a synchronous learning event (face-to-face but online). Depending on your course provider, you may also be able to speak to them on the telephone or by text according to how they want to organise things.

If you are provided with a telephone number for your tutor, you will probably also be told when they are available. This should be respected. To get the best out of a call it is a good idea to email in advance with your question(s) or concerns and arrange a mutually convenient time for the call. In this way, they will be able to prepare whatever resources they may need to help you.

Online seminars in real time (synchronous) are an important part of any course. If you are unable to attend any of the sessions, it is good practice to let your tutor know in advance. Not letting them know is the same as arranging a meeting and not turning up. They will have prepared material for a certain number of participants and so if the numbers are significantly different, the planned session may not work.

While the virtual campus is available to you 24 hours a day, seven days a week, your tutor is not.

> *I really like talking to students. That was the reason I went into teaching in the first place. We don't get much actual 'face-to-face' time during the length of the course, so we need to find other ways to break down the barriers that are caused by learning online.* (Catherine, Cambridgeshire)

The actual teaching is the best bit for me. It's so nice to be able to see my students at the tutorials. But not many of them put their webcams on. And some are reluctant to even speak and insist on writing in the chat box instead. I have no idea why! (Ralph, Bristol)

I always tell students what times I am available during the week, for instance 6pm till 8pm Monday to Friday. This is so people who are working full time can call me in the evening when they get home. The problem is though, that there are always people who ignore that and they think that because they can get all the material online day or night with the click of a mouse, that they can do the same for me! (Frances, Edinburgh)

At the beginning of the module, your tutor will also probably give you a rough guide as to how long they will take to answer emails. For instance, some might say that they hope to turn them around in 48 hours but if they are very busy this might take longer, such as when they are marking assignments.

If you do not hear back from your tutor after about a week, it is fine to contact them asking if they have received your email. It is possible your email may have gone into their Spam folder or gone astray for some other reason. To avoid this happening, you should establish contact with your tutor at the beginning of the course and make sure that all the lines of communication are working.

Some courses suggest that you upload a 'dummy' assignment through the online portal just to check that your software is compatible with the tutor's and that they will be able to read your work. This is useful because it means that you can iron out any problems in advance and not have to worry about whether or not everything will work well when the time comes to submit your assignments for marking.

After submitting course work you might become impatient, or even anxious, waiting for the results. However, there will be guidelines within which tutors work and this includes a turnaround time for assignments. This might be ten working days excluding bank holidays and other public holidays. While you are waiting, try not email your tutor and ask if they have marked your work. Most results are released in a block so all the students in the cohort get them at the same time.

Meeting other students face-to-face

Some courses are delivered through blended learning, which is a mixture of online seminars and face-to-face teaching, while others are delivered entirely online. In either case, getting to know other students on your course is a good idea. The group forum is a starting place and you could attend an open or introduction day if there is one. There may also be other formal or informal events that take place either face-to-face or online. If there is a course social media presence, you could join this or if there is not already one, you could think about setting one up. From there, it may be possible to organise some informal events.

If you decide to meet other students face-to-face, firstly be mindful of your safety and meet in a public place. A good place to meet would be at a venue where there is something you can do that relates to your course, for instance a museum, art gallery or exhibition of some kind. This breaks the ice as it is something that you will all feel comfortable doing and provides common ground to start talking to each other. This could perhaps be followed by a visit to a restaurant or café where it would be more informal.

Meeting the people that you have been, or will be, talking to in forums or in online seminars will make such a difference to your confidence levels as you are able to picture the person and how they speak. It means that it is far less likely that a misunderstanding will occur when corresponding in a written format.

Group work

Depending on what course you do, there may be an element of group work involved, where an assignment involves you working as part of a team with all the members of the team getting the same mark. This might be something like having an academic discussion about a certain topic in a forum, or it may mean jointly creating a piece of work. You might have some concerns about working with people that you do not know.

Have a look at the comments from students talking about online group work:

> *There might be some people that do not do very much and their mark will be boosted by those of us that do. Teams slow me down, I would rather work at my own pace.* (William, Cardiff)

> *I am afraid that I will hold the others back, I like to really take my time over everything so sometimes I have problems getting my work done on time.* (Eleanor, Whitstable)

> *The work might not be divided up fairly. Some students don't care about their grades but I do!* (Louise, Renfrewshire)

Groups can be put together in four ways: (a) according to the different skills of the group members; (b) the tutor making random allocations to the groups; (c) students self-organising; and (d) the tutor making specific decisions about who they think will work best with each other.

In some cases, you may not have very long to complete the task so communication is vital. It is best to start talking to your team as soon as you can. The success of a team relies on trust, shared goals and motivation.

If possible, arrange a joint Skype or Zoom call with the other members of your team right at the beginning of the task so that you can decide on a plan of action between you. Being able to see someone and hear their voice will make working with them much easier. Once you have made contact, the team can start working out a plan for who is going to do what.

Part of working in a group is reflection and so if you are doing group work as part of an assignment, it is likely that you will also be asked to write a reflection after the task has been completed. Keeping detailed notes as you go along will help enormously when it comes to doing this part of the assignment.

When online teams go wrong

Teams do not always work well together in a face-to-face environment and it can be even harder online. But the reasons why teams might not work are the same:

Problem: You do not like working in teams and get very anxious in group situations.
Solution: Contact your tutor before the start of the task and ask if there is an alternative assignment. Most course providers offer this option.

Problem: The task is not clear and people in the team disagree about what should be done.
Solution: Email your tutor and ask for clarification and then share the details with your teammates.

Problem: The planning discussions are dragging on and you are running out of time.
Solution: Take notes during the virtual meeting, or the forum discussion, and produce a list of action points for the team.

Problem: Communication is slow, with time between replies on the forum being sporadic.
Solution: Arrange an online face-to-face meeting in something like Skype or Zoom. Set up a doodle poll to see when people are available.

Problem: There is a personality clash where you feel that one member is being arrogant or rude in the way they 'speak'. Or perhaps you feel that you are not being listened to.
Solution: Before posting what could be a heated comment or sending a heated email, consider what you want to achieve. Try to arrange a time for the team to speak in 'real time' so that the tone of voice is reintroduced.

Problem: One or more members of the team have not appeared on the group forum and you do not know whether to wait for them to appear or to start work without them.
Solution: Send an email to your tutor to let them know because they will be able to make contact with the missing group member(s). In the meantime, start planning but have a contingency plan for whether or not they will appear. Do not waste time waiting.

Plan for peace

Having a plan for how you will approach any online discussion will help you work out what you are going to say and how to say it. This will help with your own confidence and lessen the chance that you may be perceived as being arrogant or rude. There are three possible approaches:

- **If you agree:** say what you agree with and why, then open it up to the whole group. For example:

    Hi [insert name]. *I really like what you say about* [...] *because* [...]. *I was also thinking that* [...]. *What do others think?*

    This acknowledges the writer and ends on a question, which opens up the discussion to the rest of the group and helps to keep the conversation going.
- **If you disagree:** provide thoughtful and constructive criticism but point out how interesting you found their approach and ask them what they think of yours. For example:

    That's a really interesting point [insert name]. *I like the way that you have approached* [...]. *I looked at this a slightly different way and thought that* [...]. *I wonder if it could be a mixture of the two?*

    This acknowledges and shows respect for the writer's point of view and opens up the discussion. Suggesting that it might be a mixture of the two shows that you are open to discussion, and you do not sound arrogant.
- **To move the discussion on:** add a new dimension to the discussion and make suggestions about how an existing point or evaluation could be expanded. For example:

    It's really interesting that we all have such different opinions on this, it has really informed my thinking. Thank you [insert name(s)]. *I've made a summary of the main points that I thought I would share if that's ok? There is another really interesting topic on page* [...]*.* *What do others think of* [...]*. I was wondering if* [...]*.*

    This demonstrates respect for everything that has been said and by summing up brings the main points together, which will be helpful for you and for the others in your group.

Summary

In many ways, learning online is similar to learning at a brick university. You will have course material to read and assignments to write. The course material may use hard copy books and a range of online materials, or perhaps consist wholly of online materials. In both these cases, it is likely that all the learning events will take place online in either a synchronous or asynchronous way. To get the best out of your course, it is good to join in with whatever you can, as soon as you can, to take some of the distance out of the distance learning.

Key points from this chapter

- Engaging with your tutor and fellow students helps to enhance the experience of online learning.
- Even though you are working online, a comfortable space to study in with a suitable chair should be arranged to avoid neck or back aches.
- Prolonged periods in front of the computer may cause eye fatigue, so regular breaks are advisable.
- Time management is important so that you do not miss learning events or the submission dates of assignments.
- Working as part of a group can be beneficial and help inform your thinking.

4 Accessing Learning and Peer Support

In this chapter you will learn about:

- the type of study skills help offered by institutions
- how to access and use online study skills support
- setting up study groups online
- how peer mentoring works.

This chapter will concentrate on where you can find out about the study skills that you need for your course and where to look for areas of support. Institutions will usually provide areas on their web pages where there is information in the form of handouts, podcasts or short exercises. There will probably also be areas on the library home page where you can book a virtual tour which shows you what sources are available and how to access them. But first, you need to know what study skills you need and this can be found in the course handbook.

The course handbook

The handbook that you receive at the beginning of your course is something that you will need to come back to again and again. It will contain a great deal of information, so it is worth downloading and filing it for easy access, or even printing off particular parts so that you can put them up on the wall near your study area. It will contain the key dates which you can put on your study calendar (see Chapter 3, *Learning in Online Environments*, for more on this).

It is a good idea to put the dates into your phone and computer calendar so that you give yourself some notice of what is coming up. For instance, you could set a notification a few weeks before an assignment is due, and then another reminder nearer the time to make sure that you do not miss the hand-in date.

The course handbook will give you an overview of what you are going to learn as the course progresses and any relevant reading lists or preparatory tasks. If there are set books that go with your course, it is a good idea to order them as soon as you can because if the course you are doing has a lot of participants from across the country, or even the world, they may end up being in short supply. Where possible, you should have a good look at them before the course starts so that you are familiar with them in advance. This will save you time later.

If you have concerns about doing the course for any reason, find the details of the Student Support Team and contact them. The details will be on your Student Home Page. They will be able to offer you support and advice which might include a student mentoring scheme where you can be matched with someone who has done the same course as you. They will be able to answer your questions and either provide or point you in the direction of resources that will help and reassure you.

Closing the gap

Distance learning can be challenging. Some of the challenges that might crop up are a feeling of isolation, lack of confidence and difficulty in maintaining motivation. As well as this, people might find that they do not have, or need to brush up on their existing study skills to be able to understand the course material and write the assignments. This might include essay writing, note taking, critical thinking, referencing or just generally how to start learning again.

The important thing to remember is that even though you may be studying alone at home, there will be a whole network of people who can help if you go get stuck. Among others, this includes tutors, learning advisors and fellow students.

Most schools, colleges and universities have a Student Support Team, so you should not feel that you are the only one who needs support. They would not need a whole department if it was only you! Support might take many different forms. For some people it will be help with things like dyslexia, and for others physical disability, mental health or other unseen difficulties (for more on this see Chapter 5, *Recognising Strengths and Overcoming Difficulties and Disabilities*).

Plan to succeed

To increase the chance of successfully completing your course, one of the most important things that you can do is to make sure you know what you have to do, how to do it and when you have to do it by. This may sound obvious, but you may not have had access to the study calendar, course material or list of assignments before you started. Once you have all this, you can start to plan how you will find the time, understand what you are learning and approach the assignments. As well as this, it is worth giving some thought to what you will do if things go wrong and you are unable to keep up for any reason.

Every year, thousands of students drop out of courses when they are faced with the first assignment. There are different reasons why this might be, for instance:

- they have not kept up with the learning and so are not able to answer the questions or do the assignment on time

- they realise that the course is not what they had expected and so feel that the first assignment is a good time to stop
- they do not understand what the question is asking
- they lose confidence and feel that they just cannot do it.

This is why a good plan for how you will get to grips with the course content right at the beginning, through the first few weeks, into the first assignment and beyond is so important.

One of the best ways to do this is to have a really good look at how the course is structured and how it will be taught. It is also useful to think about what study skills you will need to succeed and if you have those skills.

Take a look at some comments from students about getting started:

> *Make sure that you understand the requirements of your course when it comes to the assignments and where to find the resources that you might need. This information will normally be included in the introduction materials of your course.* (Maggie, Dover)

> *I think the thing that I did wrong in the beginning was not take it very seriously. I was overconfident thinking 'I can smash this!' but I soon found out that because I didn't read all the introductions to the course or have a proper look at the study planner, I struggled to get the assignment done and didn't get a very good mark in my first one.* (Arthur, Bristol)

First things first

Starting a new course is exciting. But once you start to look closely at the course material and the assignments, you may feel a little overwhelmed. This can be true even if you have enrolled in a course where the topic is something that you have studied before and know a good deal about. Alternatively, you might know little, or even nothing, about it. You may also find that you need to brush up on your study skills or even learn new ones.

At that point, you might start to worry about whether or not you will be able to complete the course, or that you will be the only one who is struggling. But remember, you are at the beginning of the course, so why *would* you be able to do it? That is the whole point of doing the course, to learn about the material, and *learn* the skills that you need to understand and apply them.

Key skills

Learning institutions usually provide a range of study skills support for their students, and in some cases this forms part of the course itself. However, this does not always happen automatically, which means that you need to recognise

Activity 4.1

Think about your experience with study skills in the areas listed below. On the figure, put the number in the area that shows how you feel about it now.

1. Learning online
2. Understanding the question
3. Academic writing
4. Referencing
5. Time management
6. Using the library
7. Creating an argument
8. Taking notes
9. Working in groups
10. Passing the course

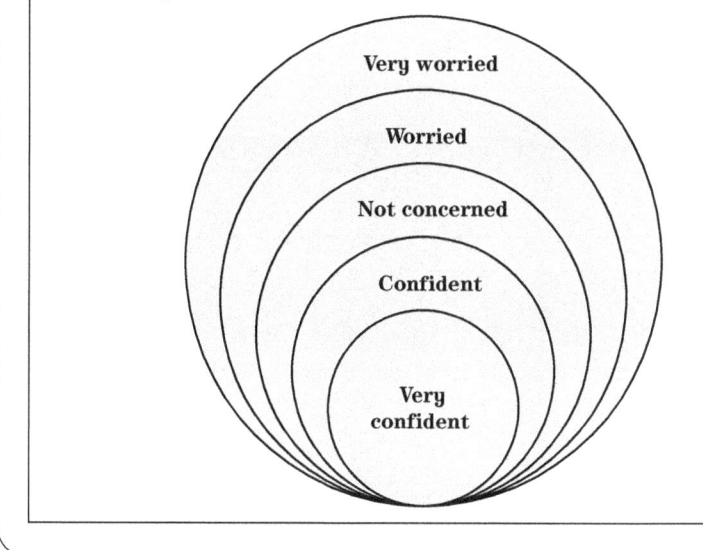

(Concentric circles labelled from outer to inner: Very worried, Worried, Not concerned, Confident, Very confident)

the type of study skills you need to work with the course material, and what skills you will need to complete the assignments.

A good way of finding out the type of study skills you are going to need is to look at the learning outcomes which will form part of the introductory material. Each course will usually have two types of learning outcomes.

Subject-specific learning outcomes

Subject-specific learning outcomes cover the factual elements that surround the topic you are studying. This knowledge will be learned from the course materials and associated activities.

Activity 4.2

Make a note below of all the things that you put in the 'worried' and 'very worried' areas. Then jot down exactly what it is that concerns you. Later, you will be able to come back to this section and note down how you are going to deal with them.

Study skill	What you are worried about?	Where to get help and support
e.g. Essay writing	How to get a solid structure	

Activity 4.3

Look at the subject-specific learning outcomes for your course. If you have them, put the details in the blank box below. If not, put in the kind of things you think it will contain. There are some examples to show you what they are usually like.

Type of course	Examples of subject-specific learning outcomes
Politics	Understand the boundaries and significance of International Relations as a sub-discipline; how globalisation impacts international politics, economics and society.
Classical Studies	An understanding of the different approaches used to work with fragmentary sources, types of archaeology and primary source texts.
Mathematics	The theory and applications of maths including statistics, algebra and trigonometry.
Your course	

Generic learning outcomes

Generic learning outcomes explain the study skills that you will need in order to understand and work with that core knowledge. In keeping with the specific learning outcomes, not all of these will be needed at once, and there may be some that apply only to specific topics or assignments. They will probably be built into the material, meaning they might be hard to spot, so it is worth doing any academic practice exercises that are signposted along the way.

The type of study skills that you might need will depend on the type of course that you are doing. For instance, if you are doing a humanities course such as English, Classics or History, you will probably be writing essays. To write these essays, you will probably need to do quite a bit of reading and note taking. Then you will use what you have found out to write some kind of analysis in a continuous prose format such as an essay.

If you are doing a social sciences course, you will probably be using case studies and statistics as your evidence, and writing an analysis of what they contain either in a prose essay format or perhaps a report.

STEM subjects such as science and maths do not normally require you to write essays. Instead, you will probably be using formulas, describing experiments or analysing a mathematical problem and its solution in a report-style assignment.

Activity 4.4

Look at the generic learning outcomes for your course. If you have them, put the details in the blank box below. If not, put in the kind of things you think it will contain. There are some examples to show you what they are usually like.

Art History	Clear essay writing which is fully referenced. Analysis of paintings and the ability to describe and analyse key features.
Classical Studies	Critical analysis of primary and secondary sources. The ability to construct scholarly writing with an appropriate academic voice.
Your course	

As well as these generic learning outcomes, individual topics and assignments may have skills that are specific to them. If you are unsure what these are, it is a good idea to email your tutor and ask their advice. The marking criteria are also a key part of the course handbook, and it is worth looking closely at the way in which marks are awarded. This information, together with the learning outcomes of the course and the guidance notes for the assignment, will give you a good idea of what you need to do in order to achieve particular grades.

Finding out all of these things is well worth doing right at the beginning of your course, so that you are clear about what to expect and what is expected of you.

Knowing what is on offer

Distance learning is becoming popular with many colleges and universities because it is a way of reaching people across the world. Some might also run the same courses on a blended or fully face-to-face basis on a brick campus. This means that the virtual campus of an institution is likely to offer a similar range of services to its online students as it does for its face-to-face students.

However, it is harder to engage with services or events when you are on your own at home and unsure how it all works. Many students, who would otherwise be confident, say that when they are faced with joining in group chats or learning events online, they struggle. This could be through lack of confidence or just not really knowing what they have to do.

You will have been given information on how to get into your Student Home Page so that you can access the learning materials, so that is the best place to start. From there, you will be able to see what else has been provided for you to help with your learning. There is likely to be a virtual tour which will help you locate everything you need to know.

Activity 4.5

Here is a list of resources that you will need to find when you first log in. Tick them off once you find them. Add in any others that you think of.

Library services		Tutor Group Forum	
Assignment questions		Health and Wellbeing Department	
Assignment submission details		Student finance	
Study skills help		Students Union	
Peer mentoring			
Student services			
Computing Helpdesk			
Course calendar			

Navigating your Student Home Page

Either when you register, or when the course you are doing starts, you will be given an academic email address that will end in something like *.ac.uk* or *.edu.com*. You will need to check it regularly, because your course provider will use it for any announcements they need to make. Having this official student email address is also useful because as a student you will be able to join the National Union of Students (NUS), which will give you discounts on a wide range of items. There are also some shops, banks, travel companies and online book sellers that offer a discount for students.

With this email address, you will receive a password and instructions on how to get into your Student Home Page for the first time. You will then be prompted to change your password to something that you will be able to remember. Remember not to use a password that you are using elsewhere because of digital security. (See Chapter 10, *Troubleshooting, Staying Safe Online*, for further details on choosing a password.)

Your Student Home Page is only a part of what you will be able to access via your login. Most, if not all, of the resources and services that you need will be available by clicking on the various links provided.

When you first log on, there will usually be some activities to get you started which will familiarise you with the website. When you have done them, they are marked as completed.

After that, perhaps spend some time looking around the various links so that you know what information they contain and where to find the services listed above and any others that you have noted down. In particular, find and bookmark where you can get study or wellbeing support if you need it.

Finding key information

On your Student Home Page, there will usually be tabs along the top of the page which will take you to different parts of the website. Clicking on the tab with the name of your course code will give you all the details of what you are going to study. It is also likely to give you information about how the course fits into wider study, for instance a specific degree. This is where there will also be a list of any set books or other equipment you may need.

The assessment tab will take you to a list of the assignment questions for your course together with guidance notes and details of how and when to submit your work. The tutorials tab will take you to a list of the online learning events and will contain details of the time and date of each class and how to access them.

There may be particular software that you need to download before you can get into the online classroom space so it is a good idea to do this in advance in case there are any problems on the day. If you do have problems with anything, you can contact the Computing Helpdesk for help.

The Resources tab will take you to a range of things that you will need to study the course. Depending on what you are studying, these might include an image gallery, academic skills activities, further reading and access to pre-recorded tutorials.

If you want to download the course content onto your desktop, laptop or tablet, you will be able to do this in different formats such as PDF or Word. Do this right at the beginning so that everything is at your fingertips and you can study wherever you are. This is one of the ways that you can take the campus with you everywhere you go.

Activity 4.6

Click on all the other tabs along the top of your Student Home Page and see what other information you can find out about your course and how it is studied. Put the phone number for the Computing Helpdesk in your notebook or phone in case you need them to help you get back into the site at some point.

Once you have finished having a good look round the homepage, return to Activity 4.5 and check that you have found everything you are likely to need. If you are worried about being able to find particular things when you come back to them, you can write down the process in your notebook. For example, to get to referencing help, you might put something like:
Library
↳ Help and Support
　　↳ Referencing
　　　　↳ MHRA Style Guide

Becoming part of the learning community

Most courses provide a way for students to interact with the others on their course. This is done in forums, synchronous (in real time) online learning events on platforms such as Blackboard, Adobe Connect or Zoom. As well as this, some courses will have induction days or day schools where you can go along and meet the tutors and some of the other students on your course. If you are not able to attend, there is often a recording put on the course website so you can catch up on what was said.

Once you have explored your Student Home Page and located the tutor group forum that is connected to your course, you will probably find that your tutor has posted a welcome message and other students have introduced themselves. It might be that there is more than one forum available to you and these are likely to connect you to the whole cohort doing your course. There may also be others on specific topics related to your field of study.

Reading these means that you are taking the first steps to becoming part of the learning community and as soon as you post something, you are making good progress. You do not have to post on, or even read, all the forums right away, as there will be plenty of time as the course progresses to do this, once you have found your feet. If you are not sure which one(s) are most important for you to be involved in, seek advice from your tutor.

A learning community does not have to be large; it can exist within your tutor group. A learning community can be created through doing three things: taking part in the same course (joint enterprise); developing an understanding of the course material (shared repertoire); and group work (mutual engagement) (Wenger, 1998, p. 73).

Participating in your own tutor group forum is probably the best place to start as it will be smaller and only those in your own group will be able to read and write to it. If you are feeling anxious about this, look back at Chapter 2 about online personas and make a plan for what you will post when you feel more comfortable.

Writing a draft message is a good step towards this and perhaps once you have seen what others are saying you will feel more confident about putting your own message up. If you are worried, have a chat with your tutor who will be able to give you some advice and they may help you to draft your first message.

It is not just other people on your course that form part of the wider learning community though. It will include the other people in the same discipline as you who are active in a more public way. For instance, they may have blogs, regularly post on Twitter or Facebook, or they may even have their own website (more on this in Chapter 9, *Using Social Media for Learning Online*). You may want to just follow them at first, but there is no reason why you cannot post things and interact with other people in your discipline like this in due course.

For instance, if you are studying Classical Studies, you could subscribe to The Conversation, which posts about what is happening in the world of Classics. It also publishes interviews with leading academics, which will give you an insight into what the main topics of debate are within the discipline.

There are similar sites for other disciplines, so if you want to follow or get involved with something like this, you could do an internet search or ask your tutor to point you in the right direction.

Becoming more familiar with what is happening in the wider learning community is a good way of making contact with others who are studying the same things as you. It also means that you can learn about the current debates in scholarship, which may well inform your thinking about your own studies.

Being an independent learner

Being an independent learner means that you need to be proactive, keeping in touch with your tutors and peers and taking responsibility for your own workload and timetable. Knowing exactly what you have to do and when you have to do it by is the first step. Once you have found this out, you can make a plan so that you do not miss any deadlines. You can also factor in the course work that you need to cover each week. Once you have all this, you can prioritise it under three headings: now, soon and later.

This kind of organisation is key to being an independent learner because it is unlikely that you will be reminded of when coursework needs to be submitted, or when there will be online learning events. All of this information will be given to you at the beginning of the course and you will be expected to find and make note of the details.

This may seem daunting at first when you are getting to grips with the material that you are studying and trying to find time to study in an already busy life. Time management is key when learning remotely because it can often be the case that spending time studying comes low down on the list of priorities for your time and energy.

Making a timetable and putting it up somewhere prominent where it can be seen both by you and the people you live with is important (for more on this, see Chapter 3, *Learning in Online Environments*). It is also useful to make yourself a priority board like the one below so that you remember everything you need to do each week.

Activity 4.7

Write in all the things that you need to do to get started for your course.

Things you need to do now	Things that need doing soon	Things that you can do later

---

To help you with this, have a good look around the website, perhaps bookmarking or writing down the areas that you think might be useful to you. This will be part of your induction, which is something that you would have as a student at a brick university. The time is not wasted, so do not be tempted to jump straight into the course material without first finding out all the things that you need to know now and what you might need to know later on.

Complete a priority board like the one above each week to make sure that you stay on track.

Peer mentoring

Can you think of anyone who has been influential in your learning? It might be a teacher from your primary school or high school, a coach or dance teacher, or maybe a family member who encouraged and supported you in everything you did. Do you ever wish that you could have something similar in terms of your online learning?

Many universities and colleges have a peer mentoring scheme where students who have done the same course as you are available to help you with various parts of your course. Naturally, they will not do the work *for* you but they will be able to guide you. They will also be able to offer you reassurance if you get worried about the course in any way.

> The hardest thing for me was being by myself all the time. I don't mean that I wanted to meet up with the others on the course or anything, just that I didn't have anyone to talk to about what I was learning and sometimes I wasn't sure if I had understood it all properly. I was matched with a mentor about half way through my second year and that made things much easier and I actually ended up enjoying the course! (Matthew, Lincoln)

It will depend on the learning institutions whether the scheme has an opt-in or an opt-out policy. If it is opt-in, you will need to actively join the scheme and you will then be matched with a mentor who will make contact with you. An opt-out scheme means that every student will be automatically matched with a mentor, and if you do not want to take part, you can just let them know.

> I wasn't all that keen on having a mentor, I thought it would be like going back to school. But one of the others on my course had one and she said that it really helped her, so I gave it a go. I was so wrong about it! My mentor was so patient and supportive, and helped me find all the help I needed to keep going. (Robert, Birmingham)

Peer mentoring has been shown to work very well and there is evidence to show that because of it many students who would otherwise have dropped out in fact stay and finish their course.

> There were a couple of times when I thought about giving up. I got to the point where I felt I just couldn't keep going. I was struggling to find time to study and that meant I got behind. In the end, I spoke to Student Services because I had decided to quit and they told me about the Students Association and the mentoring help that they offer. They were brilliant and I've almost finished my course now. (Jacquie, Westgate)

Engaging in a mentoring scheme can bring benefits at a personal, academic and vocational level. An academic peer mentoring project gives you the opportunity to work with a resourceful individual, who wants you to succeed and who can offer practical assistance and personal support to help you achieve your potential. The benefits of peer mentoring include:

- increased self-esteem, motivation and confidence
- an increased sense of direction and purpose

- the acquisition and development of study skills
- improved academic achievement
- a higher level of commitment and application to your studies
- help in combating underachievement
- the opportunity to work with a positive role model
- an increased awareness of the opportunities available to you
- an increase in employability skills.

At the end of your course, maybe you could think about becoming a mentor yourself to help new students doing the same course(s) as you. When the time comes, if you are interested, have a chat with your mentor and they will be able to talk to you about what the process involves and what type of training you would need to undertake.

Summary

The most important point to remember is that while you might be studying alone at home, there are thousands of other students out there doing the same thing. Taking whatever opportunity you can to get involved in forums, learning events or talking to your tutor will all help to take the distance out of distance learning.

Universities and colleges will have study skills information on their website and they will also have a Student Support Team who will be able to deal with any questions that you have about how to find resources.

Your tutor and others in your tutor group will also be an invaluable form of support. Your tutor will want you to succeed and to have a good experience of learning, so they will help you if they can. If they cannot, then they will explain what is available and point you in the right direction.

The others in your tutor group will all be learning online just like you and many of them will have also have questions or concerns about the course and about online learning in general. Talking to each other will be both informative and reassuring.

Becoming part of the learning community within your discipline, both at course level and more widely using social media, means that you can begin to plan what you might do with your qualification either in other parts of academia or in the world of work.

Key points from this chapter

- Get organised in advance.
- Investigate the course provider's website to see what help is available.

- Read the course handbook carefully so that you know what is expected of you.
- Discuss what you might need to brush up on with your tutor.
- Make contact with the Student Support Team.
- Communicate with your peers on course forums and other platforms.
- Do not be afraid to ask for help.

5 Recognising Strengths and Overcoming Difficulties and Disabilities

By the end of this chapter you will:

- understand what reflection is and how it benefits your learning
- know what your learning strengths are and what that means
- understand the range of assistive technologies that are available
- be able to make decisions about where and how you study
- know where to find sources of practical and financial help.

What is reflection?

Reflection is something that we do all the time without really being conscious of it. It is a part of our everyday lives no matter what we are doing. It could be about something really important, such as an educational, work, family or housing issue that we have experienced before and learned from. Or it could be something simple such as having got wet in the rain and deciding not to wear summer shoes when there are dark clouds overhead!

In most types of academic learning, you will be asked to write a reflection at some point or another. It is worth doing this even if you are not being asked to in an assignment as it helps you to be more objective about your learning journey. It is a good idea to start the process of reflection as you go along, rather than to wait and look back on what you did afterwards. A good place to do this is in a Learning Journal.

Reflection is also a really good way of keeping track of where you are now with your studying, how you are doing mentally and physically, and checking to see if there is anything else that you can do to enhance your learning, as well as your grades. Doing this will also show up areas where you could be doing better and help you plan how to make that happen.

Doing a study skills audit

Doing a study skills audit throws up areas of weakness that you need to work on but it also shows what you are good at. Too often we concentrate on the negatives, when, in fact, the things we can do well, the positives, tend to get forgotten in our haste to move forward. When starting anything new it is useful to drill down into exactly what is going to be expected of us so that help can be put into place if needed.

Start by looking at the learning outcomes for the course that you are going to do. These are skills that you will be expected to have by the end of the module. Remember, you are not expected to have them now.

So that you can assess where you are with the generic and specific skills, it is useful to carry out a skills audit at the beginning of the course to see what you need to work on. Then, as the course progresses and after each marked assignment, you should do another audit so that you can see your progression and check up on anything that you need to work on.

Activity 5.1

Study skills audit. Grade yourself in each area and then make some notes on the importance of enhancing those skills and how they relate to your work. Make a list of the specific learning outcomes for your course, grade yourself on a scale of 1–3 (with 1 being the lowest and 3 being the highest) and make some notes on how you can help make sure that you meet those objectives.

Generic study skills			
e.g. Referencing in Harvard	1	2	3

Plan

Subject-specific learning outcomes			
e.g. Be able to create a graph using statistics	1	2	3

Plan

Once you have a plan, you can factor this into your Learning Journal and check back at regular intervals to see how you are doing and if there is anything further that you need, or avenues of help that you need to pursue. This will help to make sure that you meet the skill levels needed to pass the course.

Why is it important to be reflective?

One of the best ways to make sure that you have everything you need, and that you ask the right questions when you talk to your tutor or the Student Support Team, is to be reflective as you go along. This means keeping a note of what you are studying and how you are doing it, making a note of anything you get stuck on and any questions that you want to ask.

This also means thinking about previous study you have done, what went well and not so well, how any problems were solved and what this means for starting your current course. This applies to anyone starting a course whether they have just left education, are returning to study after some time away or if they are a seasoned student.

By analysing the processes you go through in reading for and producing your academic work, you will be able to anticipate, at least to some extent, the types of issues that might come up in the future. Then you can talk to the Student Support Team about the kind of help you might need.

When should I reflect?

As your course progresses, your tutors will provide you with feedback on your assignments, and perhaps on your seminar performance. Taking time to reflect on what has been said will help to improve your skillset and ultimately your marks.

To use the feedback you receive on your assignments effectively, you could break it down into four parts.

1 What your tutor has said and what you understand it to mean.
2 Three things you have done well so that you can do them again.
3 Three things that you need to improve on so that you can do things better next time.
4 What you might need to ask your tutor or someone else.

By breaking it down like this, you will be able to create an action plan containing details of what you need to do next and where to find the resources you need.

Activity 5.2

Go through a previous assignment and check it against the questions below. This will show you what you did well and what you need to work on. N.B. Be sure to address all the issues before starting work on the next task. If you do not understand the feedback, be sure to ask your marker for clarification.

Date:
Module:
Assignment title:

Page	What your tutor says	What you understand this to mean
	e.g. Your structure is disjointed	The essay needs to flow better with smoother connections between paragraphs

Things that you have done well	
	e.g. Introduction explains the question well and shows how the essay will be structured
1	
2	
3	

Things that you need to work on	
	e.g. Making sure that all my paragraphs have a point/evidence/analysis structure
1	

2	
3	
Action plan	
	e.g. Attend an online study skills session
1	
2	
3	
Things to ask your tutor	
	e.g. Is it better to put charts in the main essay or in an appendix?
1	
2	
3	

You should also take time to reflect more widely at the end of each term so that you can see the progress you are making and highlight anything that you need to work on in time for when studying begins again.

You should also revisit your time management plan, study space and overall study habits to see what has worked well and find solutions for the things that have not worked well.

Learning difficulties

Study skills are not the only area that you should reflect on. It is also useful to think about the practicalities of studying online and whether there has been anything that might stop you from being able to participate fully. This might be something like dyslexia, dyspraxia, or needing additional support due to mental health difficulties such as depression or anxiety.

Make a specific note of this with details of the way in which it has made, or might make, studying difficult for you, or has stopped you studying particular topics in particular formats. Having this information to hand when you speak with a student advisor or your tutor will help them to help you.

Overcoming difficulties

If there is something that makes learning online difficult for you, consider what this has meant, or may mean, for your future learning. Armed with this information, you will be able to find out what is available from the course provider and other sources, which will mean that you can successfully complete the course.

> *I really wanted to do a degree but I couldn't face being in lectures with lots of people, so when my friends from school went, I stayed at home. Then someone told me about how they were studying to do a degree online. So I decided to apply and it was so much better studying at home, and I got my degree in the end!* (Valerie, Wallsend)

Activity 5.3

Make a note of anything that has made it difficult for you to study. If you are coming back into education after a break, think about things that may have caused you difficulties with studying at school or college. Then add in details of how, or if, you overcame it. If there are things that might hinder your ability to study going forward, list them here together with what you can do to overcome them or where to ask for guidance.

The problem	What this meant	How it was overcome
e.g. Dyslexia	Could not read course materials	Used coloured overlays
e.g. Anxiety	Did not attend tutorials	Watched the recordings

I was ok at university for the first few weeks, but I just got more and more anxious about having to speak in seminars. I was always worried about saying the wrong thing. I swapped to an online course and I was able to write in the chat box during classes instead. I found that much less scary. (Michael, London)

Why accessibility matters

As a society, we aim to provide access for everyone to transport and public buildings. There are hearing loops, closed captioning and many other ways in which we try to make sure that everyone has access to schools, colleges, further education and to entertainment. So why should learning online be any different?

Ability, not disability

In this chapter, we do not use the term 'disabled' or 'disability' because we believe that with the help of various technologies, everyone is 'able' to study online. And more than that, some of the assistive technologies and other resources are useful to everyone whether or not they actually 'need' them to study. For some people, being able to study online is only possible when they have the right equipment and space available to them, and some additional support if and when they need it.

Assistive technologies

Learning has never been more exciting. The ability to learn online has opened doors for thousands more people who can now take part in learning activities, gain knowledge and qualifications that may never have been possible before. Technology has revolutionised the way we learn and now we are able to learn at the touch of a button or the click of a mouse. Assistive technologies can help you progress in your studies and enjoy them along the way.

It is a good idea to speak to your course provider's Student Support Team before you pay for any software. They can advise you on what would work best for the course you are taking, and what is most suitable for you personally.

Free assistive software

It is worth asking your course provider if they have a site licence for any assistive technologies that you can use.

There is also free software that you can download. One of these is MyStudyBar at http://eduapps.org. You can use MyStudyBar straight from a USB stick if you are using a machine that is not your own or you can instal it directly to your laptop or desktop. MyStudyBar puts a whole range of individual and essential tools at your fingertips. Together, these have been designed to support the complete study cycle from research, planning and structuring to getting across a written or spoken message. MyStudyBar has six sections: each has a drop-down menu offering personal choice, flexibility and independent learning, particularly for those learners who require additional strategies to support their learning. Examples include:

- Xmind for planning and organisation
- Lingoes for when you need a talking dictionary
- LetMeType for help with text input
- Balabolka for converting text to audio and a speech-to-text app which allows you to talk to your computer.

There are always new apps coming onto the market, so it is worth looking around to see what is available. If you are not sure, ask your Student Support Team for advice.

Mental health difficulties

Whether or not you have a diagnosed mental health difficulty, taking care of your mental health is really important to help you study effectively.

> *I find it really hard to concentrate on my work when I am feeling low. I have to stop reading or whatever I'm doing. Often going for a walk helps.* (Robert, Bristol)
>
> *My tutor sends me the slides and some notes before each tutorial and sets up a chat box so that I could type any comments in during the lesson. Lots of other people started doing it as well so I felt much more confident after that.* (Maria, Basildon)

If you think that your mental health difficulties might have had, or are having, an impact on your studies, you should let your course provider know as soon as possible. They will be able to provide help and support to help you manage your studies by putting measures into place, such as:

- discussing areas of focus with your tutor
- extra time to complete your assignments
- creating a manageable study timetable
- additional support at tutorials
- taking rest breaks during exams
- taking a break from study.

There are a number of organisations aimed specifically at students which will provide you with support:

Big White Wall (bigwhitewall.com): Click on 'join us' to create an account using your college or university email. Confidential support available 24/7.

Nightline (nightline.org.uk): A listening service run by trained students offering emotional and practical information to students during the night.

Student Minds (www.studentminds.org.uk): Support for mental health of university students for themselves, a friend or loved one.

Learning styles and strengths

The equipment that you need and how you set up your learning plan, learning environment and study space will depend on what your learning style and strengths are. Therefore, it is a good idea to think about this first.

Each one of us learns in a different way. We do this because of the way that our brain is wired. Activity 5.4 will help you identify the type of learner you are likely to be. Some people fall neatly into one category or another, or you may find that you fit into different categories in equal measure. Either way, this does not necessarily mean that you cannot try out other methods to see if they work for you. There are three types of learners: visual, auditory and kinaesthetic.

Activity 5.4

What are your learning strengths? What kind of learner are you? You might have more than one answer for each question. Circle all the answers that you think most apply to you.

1. **When I am learning something, I learn it by:**
   a. watching someone do it
   b. being told how to do it
   c. having a go at it myself

2. **When I check my spelling, I:**
   a. look at the word to see if it looks right
   b. sound the word out in my head
   c. get a feeling about whether it is right

3. **If someone asked me for directions, I would:**
   a. draw them a map
   b. explain how to get there
   c. point towards where they should go

4. **When I have to remember a list of things, I:**
   a. write them down
   b. repeat them to myself a few times
   c. say them as I count them off on my fingers

> **5. When I am working out how to solve a problem, I:**
> a. draw a mind map or plan of some kind
> b. think the various strategies through
> c. do some kind of physical activity as I think
>
> **6. When I work with figures or do any maths, I:**
> a. can see by looking at them whether it is right
> b. add the figures up in my head or out loud
> c. write the sum out again to check it
>
> **7. When remembering people's names, I:**
> a. remember people's faces easier than names
> b. remember people's names easier than faces
> c. remember the details of meeting them easier than their names
>
> **8. When working on something, what helps me most is:**
> a. when the room is tidy
> b. the room is quiet
> c. the chair feels comfortable
>
> **Results:** Write in how many of each letter you circled:
>
> a: _____ b. _____ c. _____
>
> Now turn to Appendix 2 at the back of the book, have a look at the letter that you scored most of and read what it says about your learning style and strengths. But consider the other learning styles as well and try anything that you think might work as well, or better, than what you are already doing. Some people have a blend of one, two or even all three types of strengths, and that is absolutely fine!

Once you have identified your learning style and strengths, you can think about how you can apply these to your online course. A lot of the learning materials will be digital but this does not mean that they are not available in different formats.

If your strength is in handling the material, and perhaps writing notes or diagrams on it, then you should explore the possibility of obtaining hard copy resources if your course material is wholly or partially online. It is also possible to translate your learning strengths into a digital format. For instance:

- As a visual learner, your learning strengths are seeing and reading, so the best online format for you would be things like maps, films, flow charts, written sources and diagrams. The best kind of technology for visual learners is software that highlights the words as they are read out. For example,

NaturalReader is a text-to speech app that reads web pages, documents and eBooks aloud with a natural-sounding voice.

- As an auditory learner, your learning strengths are listening and speaking, so the best online formats for you are seminars, discussions, listening to recordings of the classes and live online chats. The best kind of technology for auditory learners is software that converts text to speech such as WordTalk, which is a toolbar add-on for Word, or Capti Voice if you are working on a Mac.
- As a kinaesthetic learner, your learning strengths will be hands-on, practical tasks. The best kinds of online format include simulations, case studies or live and recorded tutorials. The best kind of technology for kinaesthetic learners is recording software to listen while doing other things such as podcasts and other recordings and playbacks.

The format of course material

Now that you know what your learning strengths are, you will find it easier to decide which format is best for you to be able to learn effectively.

Most online course providers have a print on request service where they will provide you with a printed copy of the online course material. This will usually come with a spiral binding so that the pages can be turned easily.

If, for instance, you have been diagnosed with dyslexia, you could also request that the course provider print on pastel coloured paper so that it is easier to see what has been written.

> It took a while for the printed course material to arrive so in the meantime I printed off what I needed on pastel paper which made it easier for me to read. I've got everything I need now so I can join in the forum discussions with the rest of my group. (Andrew, Dover)

> Because I have trouble seeing, I have software which reads the computer page to me so I can keep up with the reading. I dictate my essays and upload them onto the system to be marked. It works really well. (Robert, Newcastle)

If the course material you receive is printed on white paper, coloured overlays or coloured reading rules might be useful if you experience visual stress. Many people find that it is uncomfortable to read black text on white paper. The reasons for this could be due to a specific learning difficulty (SpLD), which is a difference or difficulty with some particular aspect of learning, or it could simply be that reading black text on white paper is harsh on the eyes. Whatever the reason, it is worth exploring ways of making things easier and more comfortable to manage.

Studying online with dyslexia

The most common learning difficulties are dyslexia, dyspraxia, attention deficit disorder/attention deficit (hyperactivity), dyscalculia and dysgraphia. Approximately 1.5 million people in the United Kingdom are affected by one of these conditions (Office for National Statistics, 2019). This figure may be even higher because some people do not talk about the problems they experience with reading, or in some cases, may not even realise that they are having issues.

If you have a diagnosis for any of the above, or if you suspect that you might be affected, you should let your course provider know so that they can look into ways of providing appropriate help and support. It is very common to have an overlap of some of these conditions.

Dyslexia can cause problems with reading, writing and spelling but does not affect a person's intelligence in any way. This can make it extremely frustrating because you know what it is that you want to write but find yourself making simple errors that you have little control over.

Dyslexia may be an obstacle, but it does not have to be a limitation. The brains of children and adults with dyslexia simply interpret information differently. There are plenty of resources available to help you reach your full potential regardless of whether it hinders your reading, writing, spelling and sometimes speaking.

Student Support Teams should be your first port of call if you are, or suspect that you might be, dyslexic. They will also be able to arrange for you to have a test if you need one together with specific advice about what tools are most suitable for the type of course you are taking.

> *I really struggled using a computer or tablet because the letters just kept jumping around, so I never thought I would be able to do an online course. But now I have a coloured screen and tinted glasses and I can read and write on the screen really easily!* (Martin, Middlesbrough)

> *I have been using coloured overlays since I was at school so I am used to them really. When I started my online course, I found that coloured glasses were easier for me than using a coloured slide on the screen and overlays on my books. They work really well and I can study on my tablet or phone without having to worry about installing any software.* (Stephen, Canterbury)

Coloured overlays

Coloured overlays are a very effective way of making reading easier. You may already have been assessed for what colour works best for you. If you are unsure about this, you can buy a set of coloured overlays to try before you invest in a coloured ruler which attaches to your book or paper.

For reading on the screen there are many free programmes called SS overlays that are available to help change the colour of your computer monitor to a colour that makes it easier for you to see it.

Another possibility is a T-bar set up where you have a colour ruler or rulers of varying widths and heights. You can move them up and down via the cursor so that you can read and/or write against the coloured band.

The same type of thing, but one that colours your whole screen, is available to buy and instal for most computers running Windows 7 or later. This allows you to test out the various colours until you find the one that works best for you. In some cases, you can purchase tinted glasses with appropriate lenses from your optometrist.

Visual stress

Dyslexia and visual stress (VS) are not the same. Visual stress affects the way that you perceive whatever you are looking at. It is not related to vision itself, and so is not relieved by prescription glasses. Some of the symptoms that you might notice when working online are:

- text jumping around on screen
- swirling effects or shimmering colours
- the background becoming more prominent than the text
- double vision, fading or blurring of text
- headaches and eyestrain associated with reading
- text appearing blurred or going in and out of focus
- text appearing double or alternation between single and double
- difficulty keeping your place in text
- difficulty tracking across lines of text
- text that appears to shimmer.

If you are experiencing any of these symptoms, you should make an appointment with an optometrist to have your eyes tested to rule out any underlying medical cause. They may also be able to advise you on other ways to relieve the symptoms.

The most common way to deal with visual stress is to use a coloured overlay or change the colours of the background screen of your PC or tablet to a pale pastel colour. This will relieve the strain on your eyes which causes the effects that stop you from being able to see the letters and words on the screen, or on the page, clearly.

Visual stress stems from a processing issue which is triggered by sensitivity to light, made worse by the glare caused by having black lettering on a white background. It is very common, with about 20% of the general population affected to some degree or other. It can make it difficult to read and it is estimated that 40% of those who struggle with reading suffer from this condition. As with dyslexia, this condition often goes undiagnosed as people may think that their eyes are tired from spending too much time in front of a screen or reading.

Most people who suffer from visual stress find that filtering out some of the reflected white light by reading through a tinted transparent overlay has the effect of slowing down the nerve cells and removing the disturbing after-images from the text.

Speech-to-text and vice versa

It is still possible to study online even with varying degrees of visual impairment. This is done through the use of adaptive technologies such as screen magnifiers or screen readers. Screen readers convert text on a screen into speech.

Your computer may have a built-in feature that allows you to dictate onto the screen. This is one of the easiest ways of writing your course work and communicating with other people online.

There are also a number of free apps that you could try such as Dragon Dictation, Speech-to-Text, Evernote and ListNote. These programs all transform your speech into the written word but it is worth trying different ones until you find the one that works best for you. Note that with some assistive technologies like these, you will need to say the punctuation out loud, and with others you will have to put the punctuation into the keyboard as you go along.

If your computer has a speech-to-text program, it is likely that it will also have a screen reading facility. Text-to-speech programs work in a similar way to speech-to-text programs. They read the screen out loud. Additional software will be needed if you need to hear what keys you are typing into your keyboard.

This is the kind of software that can often be provided by your college or university or purchased independently. These types of assistive technologies are the kind of thing that an award of additional funding (such as DSA in the UK) could be used for.

Using software to create a visual plan

For visual learners, creating a plan on the screen using the in-built tools can make it much easier to map out the plan for an assignment. It can also help with keeping track of the word count so that you do not go over the limit set for your assignment. Seeing the plan develop makes it easier to follow and to see connections between the various parts of the argument.

For instance, using the Smart Art feature in Word, you can create a variety of shapes to show the relationship between your ideas. Creating a plan like this makes it easier for you to plot out the main points that you want to make. You can also see how they come together to form the conclusion.

There are also additional technologies that you can download to create mind maps that can help you put together a lot of ideas in one place. These can be useful for essay planning but they can also be a useful way of collating your notes so that you can see the topic in one place and see the connections between the various parts.

If your strength is in being a visual learner, this kind of software can be particularly useful because it allows you to categorise and colour code all the information you input. This will allow you to see how all the individual parts of a main idea work together as a whole.

There is some free software available online but, as with anything else that you might download onto your computer, phone or tablet, you should check first to make sure that it is a legitimate site, so ensuring that you do not download a virus onto your device.

Creating a mind map on a single page means that you can view several pages alongside each other on your screen at any given time and work from them onto another document when doing written assignments.

A good way of creating a more visible form of a lecture or seminar discussion is to listen back to the recording and create a mind map from what was said. You can stop and start the recording as you go so that you do not miss anything. The advantage of doing this is that you do not have to put in everything that was said, but instead simply include the most important points.

Blind or partially sighted

If your sight is restricted, even if only you use glasses or contact lenses, you may need extra resources and to create an alternative plan so that you can study. You may already be registered as sight impaired (partially sighted) or severely sight impaired (blind) and have either a letter or a card which confirms this that you can provide when applying for an online course.

You might need very little in the way of adaptation, or you may need to use very different methods because you have no vision at all. It is useful to ask yourself the following questions:

- Can you read well at a reasonable speed, even if you are using things like a magnifier, glasses, extra lighting or other devices?
- Can you see enough of the screen to use a computer, even if you need a large screen, or do you have to make changes to it such as enlarging the text or putting on coloured overlays?

If the answer is 'yes' to either of these two questions, you should ask your course provider for the course material to be sent to you in large print, in braille and/or emailed to you as PDFs that you can enlarge with computer software. If the answer to the questions is 'no', then you will need your course materials in a non-visual format. This might involve using audio recordings and screen reading software.

Most course providers are able to offer a Digital Accessible Information System (DAISY), which is a worldwide digital reading format that combines audio, text and graphical information in one package. This makes it accessible to a wide range of people whose text reading ability might be affected by sight restrictions, or some other issue such as dyslexia.

Table magnifier

Table magnifiers, or visualisers, may help with your reading whether or not you are sight impaired. There is a range of different types of table magnifiers to choose from. These can either stand over or in front of your books, or be on a flexible arm that you can angle yourself.

There are some table-top magnifiers that have a stand or you can attach them to your desk. Ideally, they should also contain a light to enhance visibility. They will usually plug into your device using a USB cable or into the mains socket.

These are extrememly useful if you suffer from any kind of sight loss or just need the text to be a bit bigger so that you can see it more clearly. They can also be used in conjunction with coloured overlays for extra clarity.

Deaf or hard of hearing

Being deaf or having partial hearing loss does not mean that you cannot study online, or in a brick university. When you study online, the course materials will be in writing for the most part, and most providers also include a transcript of any audio or visual content. If these are not supplied, you should ask the Student Support Team for advice. They may be able to have the source converted into a format that will allow you to access it.

> *I use British Sign Language (BSL) but I do not expect my tutor and peers to know it. I found that during tutorials, I could lip-read but I could not take notes at the same time. I had to watch the recording back and pause it in places so that I could write things down. It took a bit longer but it was worth it because going over it a second time gave me a better understanding of what we had talked about than it did the first time. I put this in a post on the forum and now others are doing the same thing as me even though they don't have any problems with their hearing!* (Calia, Portsmouth)

There may be times when you need to attend synchronous tutorials with your tutor and fellow students. To enable you to fully participate, you should ask your tutor if they can provide you with the slides, handouts and additional notes in advance.

During the tutorial itself, it is likely that there will be a chat box where the discussion takes place, and again, you should email your tutor to help work out a way that you can fully participate. Among the options are that people could type while they are talking or if you are able to lip-read, you will be able to follow what is happening if fellow learners are using their web cams.

If there are actual (as opposed to virtual) face-to-face tutorials on your course, there will probably be a hearing loop at the venue, so you should let your tutor know in advance that you will need to use it. They can arrange for a portable induction loop and microphone audio source to be available for you.

If you have been awarded a grant to help you study, the college or university may be able to provide a note taker for you or you could bring along a friend or family member to do it for you. It is customary to let your tutor know in advance if you are going to do this.

Studying can take more time if you are deaf and having to read transcripts of audio materials, especially if they contain words that you are unfamiliar with. This is particularly true if you are studying a science or mathematics-based course. If this is the case, you should email your tutor and ask them to explain the things that you do not understand.

If you have previously notified the college or university that you have reduced hearing, your tutor will have been made aware and will be ready to make reasonable adjustments to their teaching. Be sure to have a discussion with them as soon as the course begins so that material and tutorial delivery can be adjusted as necessary.

Developing your confidence

If you are new to learning online and have an additional support need, it may feel overwhelming to be faced with all the different technologies that are available to you. You have taken the first step and are gathering the information that you need to get started by reading this book. Remember, you do not need to use any or all of what is available, and you can make decisions about what works best for you.

The online environment can be confusing at times and almost everyone, at some point, needs help adjusting to learning online. The problem that most people have with asking for help is that they equate it with weakness. But you have made a commitment to study online and are, no doubt, working hard. And there may well be times when you have looked at your options, and tried to find a solution for yourself, but cannot. This is when to ask for help. This can be via email or phone to your tutor or Student Support Team, whichever you feel most comfortable with.

The important thing to remember is that you are not alone. Thousands of students every year need additional support with their studies. And every year, thousands of students successfully complete their studies as a direct result of asking for, and receiving, help.

Planning ahead

Often the fear of the unknown is worse than the thing itself, so a good way to help to develop your confidence is making a plan of what you are going to do and how you will do it. In this way, you are taking control of what needs to be done, rather than it taking control of you.

> **Activity 5.5**
>
> Using the form below, write down any questions that you need to ask in terms of assistive technologies or things that you need to find out before you start studying, and any action that you need to take. Come back to this activity later to tick them off and add any more that you have thought of.
>
> | Question | Action | By: date | Done |
> |----------|--------|----------|------|
> | | | | |
> | | | | |
> | | | | |
> | | | | |
> | | | | |

Summary

Studying online when you have any kind of additional support needs requires careful planning. Make sure you discuss any additional support you *might* need with the course provider before signing up to an online course.

Most colleges and universities have a dedicated department full of people who are specialists in helping students to get the best out of their courses. They will know what equipment is available to you and how to access it. They will be able to help you apply for sources of funding to pay for resources over and above what they can provide in the normal course of events.

If you do not qualify for additional financial help, there are numerous sources of free software that can help with colouring the screen, text-to-speech and speech-to-text. It is worth exploring all possibilities.

Key points from this chapter

- Recognising your learning strengths can help you establish what kind of studying is best for you and will provide you with a range of methods to try.
- It is worth trying out alternative ways of working so that you find the ones that are best for you.
- Your course provider will have a range of strategies to make sure that their courses are as accessible as possible. You should let them know if there is anything that might have an impact on your ability to study so that they can help.
- There is a range of free software available online, ranging from screen readers to coloured overlays. You could also speak to your optometrist about the possibility of coloured glasses.

6 Academic Integrity and Employability

In this chapter you will learn how to:

- create and maintain a professional online presence
- develop effective relationships with your course leader
- showcase your skills to prospective employers
- develop an academic voice.

The challenges of online learning

Not being physically present creates a number of challenges and this requires a new skillset. No matter how tech-savvy we might be, the interaction that takes place when learning online is not a form of social media, and it should not be assumed that the two are interchangeable with people moving smoothly and comfortably between them.

Having an online presence in addition to a face-to-face presence at work is new for many people. Increasingly, companies are asking their employees to do Continuing Professional Development (CPD) courses online. This is because it is often more economical and takes less time from the working week than sending employees to another location to be trained. Some of these courses might be done alone, but others might involve remote group working and/or forum discussions.

This means that you need to develop a new skillset: firstly, the skill of learning online with all the technical challenges that might present, and secondly, being able to write succinctly and professionally with peers and possibly managers. Equally important is developing the *confidence* to do this.

> I was fine in the office and talking to people face-to-face, but when it came to working online, I was not really sure how to address people. I would normally just say 'hello' but when I start a conversation online it feels like I should be saying something more. (Robert, Client Services)

> I talk to people a lot online for work, so when it came to doing the course, it was fine until I had to start doing assignments. This is something I haven't done since I was at school. I didn't realise how different doing a course and going back to being a student would be from my normal day-to-day job. (Dan, Logistics Manager)

Despite perhaps already having some experience and knowledge in your professional field, once you are involved in online learning, you become a student, and it is the expectation of your employer or those organising the course that you will participate fully. Therefore, you need to develop a new element to your workplace identity, a student identity, one that is willing to listen, and to learn. There may not be any formal assignments but there is usually some way of evaluating your progress at the end of the training which may be challenging.

Developing an academic self for the workplace

When you consider the number of 'selves' you already have in your day-to-day life, developing an academic identity is not unachievable. There is the 'self' that you have at home and with those closest to you; the 'self' that you present when in social situations outside the home; 'the self' you have when interacting with strangers; and the 'self' you have in the workplace.

Although there is of course part of you that stays the same across all of these, there will be changes to the way in which you speak, the words that you use and the way that you use them, according to where you are and who you are with.

There are also the online 'selves' and you might have any or all of these. An online presence through work is one where an employer has details of their employees online for potential clients to see. This is fairly static and within a traditional framework set by the web page designer.

Another type is a CV-style 'self' on a site such as LinkedIn where you are making yourself visible to potential employers and where you showcase the particular characteristics relevant to your career path. You might also use a platform like this as a place to network with other people in the same profession.

Another type of online 'self' might be on a platform such as Twitter where you present a more comprehensive view of who you are, with your interests and opinions visible to everyone. These often have the disclaimer 'all opinions are my own and not my employer's' as a way of separating your work self and the personal self. However, this remains a very visible platform and things you say here can have an impact on the way you are seen in your work life.

Another 'self' is on a platform such as Facebook where you might put more personal details about you and your life, and one which you can allow a limited number of people to see if you choose. Because Facebook can feel very informal and as if you are talking to friends and likeminded individuals, it is easy to relax to the point where you upload the kinds of things that might be embarrassing, or may even damage your career prospects, in years to come.

All these selves are under your control and you can choose how to appear within them.

Working in a new space

No matter how experienced you are in any or all of the different online spaces, when starting an online course you might find that you are nervous about stepping into a new, unknown type of medium and one about which you know very little. The topics you will be expected to discuss either in person by communications such as Skype, Zoom or Microsoft Teams, or in writing via a forum, and probably in assignments of some kind, may also be new to you. This may make you feel nervous because you are worried about saying something that is wrong in front of a group of people that you do not know, not being able to keep up or not finding the time to contribute to forums.

Activity 6.1

Make a list of the different online spaces that you use to communicate with other people, e.g. Facebook or Twitter. Rate yourself from 1 to 3 (with 1 being the lowest and 3 being the highest) on how comfortable you are in that medium.

Name of the online space	1	2	3

Activity 6.2

If you scored yourself low on any of the platforms that you use, what are the steps that you could take to increase your confidence? Jot down some ideas in the box below.

The other problem that might occur is that someone else on the course is very vocal, taking up most of the time in the synchronous discussions (learning events that happen in real time) and then going on to write lots of long posts on the asynchronous forums leaving nothing else for the rest of the group to say (see Chapter Two, *Online Identity and Personas*, on how to deal with this situation).

Becoming part of an academic community now that you are studying is very much like joining any other kind of club. You will soon get to know people, the way things work and the skills you need to use, or learn, along the way to communicate in this new way. Therefore, developing an 'academic self' that goes alongside your workplace identity is something that will probably come naturally to you as long as you engage as fully as you can with any welcome threads, pre-course activities and getting to know the course leader.

Online learning for Continuing Professional Development

It is easy to forget that those who have written and those who teach and assess online courses are real people who just happen to stay behind the scenes in some cases, and who are available at the click of the mouse in others. The people who teach online courses, however, *are* real people who have a good deal of knowledge about the topic and want to pass this on to you. Perhaps they have a real passion for the subject and want you to fall in love with it too, or perhaps it is a straightforward set of information that you need to know for a specific purpose. But do not forget that they will have chosen to teach the course and will have probably undergone training on the material and how to deliver it.

If there is an assignment element to the course, it is important to trust and use their feedback. You will probably have the right to appeal a mark if you are very unhappy with it, but in general, you should trust their judgement when it comes to marking your assignments. They will know the learning outcomes inside out and will have seen countless assignments on the topic. This is all part of allowing yourself to be a student who is being taught and who is learning.

Getting to know the group they are teaching allows course leaders to be both proactive and reactive. Shortly before, or perhaps at the very beginning of the course, you will receive a welcome email from the course leader introducing themselves. And if some or all of the course material involves the use of printed materials, you may well also receive a hard copy welcome letter.

This means that the course providers will be able to deliver the content in such a way that the group will find it easier to comprehend. In turn, this will make the material more accessible and easier for you to understand. Therefore, responding to this first contact is important for both you and them.

Not only that, but it is also bad manners not to respond to someone who is introducing themselves to you. If they were speaking to you face-to-face, you would not ignore them! Just because the course is online, and the course leader is behind a computer screen, it does not mean that normal rules of social engagement should be ignored.

The welcome email will probably be the first contact that you have with the 'teacher' and it will usually contain details of how and when the teaching will take place, how and when they will contact you, and how and when you can contact them. Do not forget that although they are part of the online delivery of the course, it does not mean that they are available 24 hours a day in the same way that the online material is.

Like you, they will have an academic self, their work self, and beyond that, again just as you do, they have a life they are living beyond the screen. It is very easy to forget that they are 'real people' and see them as part of the website rather than existing outside it. So just because you are up early, or working late, it does not mean that you can or should contact them by phone or text outside of normal working hours.

No one appreciates getting a text at midnight or a telephone call at 7am on a Sunday morning! If you do want to make contact outside hours, it is best to send an email.

Getting to know the course leader

Getting off on the right foot at the start of your course is important. You will probably already be very busy, so fitting in a course on top of everything else that you no doubt have to do and no matter how much you want to allocate time to studying, it can be difficult. Making time to get started at the very beginning is a good way of feeling that you are in control, even if there are times later on when you need to catch up a bit.

> I had to do a CPD course for work and it said that it had 12 contact hours. I didn't realise that it meant 12 actual hours online in actual sessions with the trainer and then more hours doing group work in a forum as well as writing a report at the end. It was really hard to find the time to do it all and in the end I had to email the trainer and ask for help. He was great and helped me get back on track so I could finish the course. (Phillip, Engineer)

> It turned out that two of the other people who were on the course were from a company I used to work for. I had also met the trainer a couple of years ago when she did a health and safety inspection visit to where I work, so I wasn't worried about talking in the online face-to-face sessions or in the forums. She suggested that I make a professional online profile so I could link up with other people in the same job as me. (Dee, Health and Safety Manager)

A good way to get started is with an email to the course leader or if they have already sent out a welcome email, respond to that. Breaking down the anonymity as soon as possible makes a lot of difference to the way in which you can engage with the course. Getting to know the course leader and, if possible, some of the other people on the course will make you feel far more comfortable.

Being nervous or worried about working with people that you do not know can have an effect on how well you do in the course. So it really is worth replying to the initial email, and indeed any subsequent emails from your course leader, to say something about yourself and why you have chosen to study the course.

> One of the most difficult things from a trainer's point of view is that I cannot get to know the participants if they will not meet me halfway by joining in on the forum and answering my emails! The other thing that I have to do is to try and get people to enjoy the online group work. Most people are used to working as a team in other parts of their lives but it is different and probably more difficult online as they do not know each other. That is why I create some social type threads at the beginning and some kind of icebreaker exercise just like I do in the 'real life' classroom. (Lee, HR Consultant)

The course leader will welcome your response because they, too, want to develop a good working relationship with the cohort they are teaching. This is probably the first contact you will have in regard to the course since you enrolled, so it should be an exciting time. It is also the time in which you start to develop your academic identity, so it is worth thinking about how you want to be perceived (more on this in Chapter 2, *Online Identity and Personas*).

Getting started: Meeting your peers

Imagine going along to a meeting where everyone had a paper bag over their head, where no one was allowed to speak and the only way to communicate was by passing notes. This is what it can feel like when you are learning online – so it is really important to get involved in the discussions as soon as you can.

At the beginning of any course, there will probably be a welcome thread started by the course leader introducing the material, saying a bit about themselves and inviting the learners to do the same. You might have logged on right at the beginning and be one of the first to post a message, or it may be that by the time you log on there is already a lively conversation taking place. Whichever the case, deciding what to say about yourself can be difficult and perhaps even a bit nerve-wracking, or perhaps you are used to talking to others online and feel very confident. Either way, it is worth giving some thought to what you are going to say and how you are going to say it, because in many ways conversations in an academic forum are different from those you might have been involved in before, perhaps on social networks.

How you present yourself online is particularly important if you want to develop your career. Online networking and a good formal identity is becoming more and more important when looking for jobs. Employers will often do a search in order to find out as much as they can about potential employees.

Activity 6.3

Have a look at any searchable online profiles that you have on social media. What information do they give about you?

Information	Yes	No	Information	Yes	No
Full name			Where you work		
Date of birth			If you like your job		
Where you were born			Your political position		
Where you live now			Your last holiday		
Marital status			Family photos		
Name of your partner			Hobbies		
Number of children			Social habits		
Names of children					
Number of/name of your pets					

If you were surprised by how much information you are giving about yourself, you may want to adjust the privacy settings on your online accounts or delete some of the content. It is also a good idea to ask people not to tag you in their photos on their social media. In this way, you can contain and control your online profile as much as possible.

If for any reason there is anything about you that can be found in a Google search that you feel could have a negative impact on your life, or the life of your family, you can ask for it to be deleted. However, going forward, it is advisable to limit any personal information put on social media to your family and closest friends.

When joining a thread, the first words you type will be the equivalent of the first impression you give when walking into a room and speaking for the first time. In a situation like that, you would not ignore the other people already there, instead you would acknowledge them before joining in and your language, vocabulary and tone would be appropriate to the situation.

Have a look at the discussion below:

Lee (moderator): *Hi Everyone and welcome to the course. I'm Lee and I am the course-coordinator for this module. I would like to use this thread for us to get to know each other a little bit before all the hard work begins! I live in Bournemouth and enjoy getting out into the countryside as much*

92 A Student's Guide to Online Learning

as I can. I am looking forward to 'meeting' you all and working with you. Please say a little bit about yourselves and why you are taking this course. Over to you!

Jaiden: *Hi Lee and all my fellow students. My name is Jaiden and I live in Liverpool. I am really excited about this course – I am especially excited about doing the joint project over the summer. I can't take time off to study full time so this course is perfect for me because it fits around my job and family. I look forward to meeting you all!*

Marshall: *Hi everyone. Great to be here. I have had a quick look at the course materials and they look good but a bit difficult in places! I'm hoping that there will be lots of discussions on the forums so that we can help each other out, I for one am going to need all the help I can get!* ☺

Joshua: *I'm only doing this course so I can get promoted. I just want to get it out of the way as quickly as I can.*

The first three are quite friendly, but you might think the last post seems rather abrupt, even rude but without the tone of voice or facial expression, it is impossible to tell. Look at the alternative below:

Joshua: *I'm only doing this course so I can get promoted. I just want to get it out of the way as quickly as I can.* ☺ ☺ ☺

As you can see, the way a post can 'sound' is very different once some emoticons have been added. Note that the course leader has said something about herself and has asked the group specific questions, so the easiest thing to do is to follow the same pattern.

Activity 6.4

Have a go at writing a post in response to Lee's message above. Introduce yourself, say why you are doing the course, and a little bit about yourself

---

It may seem like a waste of time getting to know people that you are never going to meet but in fact the opposite is true. The communications you have with your peers while doing online elements of a course are in fact a very important part of the whole learning process.

Learning is not just about training, books, coursework and certificates, but also about being able to articulate what you have learned and apply it to other relevant situations in your life. But more than that, the contacts that you interact with online in a study capacity often become part of your professional network later. Therefore, it is doubly important to interact in a professional way.

Personal branding

Looking around at people in the streets as you walk along, what do you see? There will be people in jeans, shorts, suits, smart and casual clothes, and it all makes an impression on us. No matter how non-judgemental we think we are, everyone makes split-second judgements about other people because of the way they look and what they wear.

That judgement might just fleet across our minds but if we never interact with the people we see, we would probably never give it another thought. But if we did happen to speak to that person again in another context, that impression might stay the same or it might change. Let us say, for instance, that as you pull into the car park at work, a man in a pair of shorts is locking up his pushbike. You might not take a lot of notice of him and if you do speak to each other, it would be a fairly relaxed conversation between two peers.

However, if you were to go into a meeting and meet the same person for the first time, this time in a much more formal setting and he is wearing a suit and chairing an important meeting, you would probably have a totally different impression of him. The way you speak to him, and the language you use, would probably also be different because of the formality of the occasion, which may well have its own set of 'community discourse' language suitable to that situation.

The opposite is also true and you might meet someone in a well-cut suit with whom you feel you should be very formal, but who is in fact a fellow worker, who you know well, who just happens to be dressed very smartly. The point is that even when you are face-to-face, it is not always easy to know who you are talking to.

It is much harder online when you have no way of seeing and sometimes not even knowing who you are talking to. This is why it is good to develop an academic voice when studying or completing training online as it has its own set of rules, and then you cannot go wrong.

Creating your brand

We have already looked at the different kinds of 'self' that you might have online and how, when you start studying, you will start to create an academic 'self' within the context of your course (see Chapter 2, *Online Identity and Personas*, for finding the right voice when learning online). If you do not already have a professional online presence, you might want to think about creating a profile to make yourself more visible in the employment and academic world so that you can showcase your achievements. In this case, you will again need to think carefully about how you want to be perceived.

Start by choosing a profile photo. An avatar might be acceptable to use in less formal circumstances but in order to make the best impression, and appear open and approachable, a profile photo is much better. Choose something that is fairly recent and has a high resolution so that it uploads well and looks sharp.

Activity 6.5

Rate your confidence levels against each of the criteria (with 1 being the lowest and 3 the highest).

Graduate skill	Definition	Score 1	2	3
Verbal communication	the ability to express ideas clearly and confidently in speech			
Teamwork	being able to work confidently within a group			
Commercial awareness	being able to see the 'bigger picture', the realities affecting the organisation			
Analysing and investigating	gathering information to establish facts and principles, problem solving			
Initiative/ self-motivation	being able to act on initiative, identify opportunities and being proactive in putting forward ideas and solutions			
Drive	a determination to get things done, making things happen and looking for better ways of doing things			
Written communication	the ability to express yourself clearly in writing			
Planning and organisation	able to plan activities and carry them through effectively			
Flexibility	being able to adapt to changing situations and environments			
Time management	managing time effectively, prioritising tasks and working to deadlines			

Adapted from Frith, May & Pocklington (2017, p. 83).

In the photo, you should be facing the camera, smiling and wearing formal or semi-formal clothes, the kind of thing that you might wear in the workplace. A prospective employer does not want to see your holiday snaps! LinkedIn (2021) warn that 'unprofessional photographs can damage your credibility and your personal brand preventing people from connecting with you'.

Next, think about the key skills that are needed in your prospective employment area. If you have just finished university and are applying for further

Activity 6.6

Have another look at the graduate skills that employers want and thinking widely about your life experience as well as your working life, write down examples of where and how you meet the criteria.

Graduate skill	Definition	Example(s)
Verbal communication	the ability to express ideas clearly in speech	
Teamwork	being able to work confidently in a group	
Commercial awareness	recognising the realities affecting the organisation	
Analysing and investigating	gathering information, facts and problem solving	
Initiative/self-motivation	being able to act on own initiative, being proactive	
Drive	making things happen and looking for better ways of doing things	
Written communication	the ability to express ideas clearly in writing	
Planning and organisation	able to plan activities and carry them through	
Flexibility	being able to adapt to changing situations	
Time management	managing time effectively, working to deadlines	

Adapted from Frith, May & Pocklington (2017, p. 84).

education, think about any previous employment, work experience or volunteering that you have done that is relevant. Think about any clubs or societies that you belong to and if there is a way that you can use them to demonstrate your suitability for the career path you want to follow.

If you are already in employment and want to use the qualification you are studying to update your CV, think carefully about the different roles within your chosen industry and how you can demonstrate your employability.

Based on a number of surveys on the skills required by employees undertaken by a range of large corporations such as Microsoft, the BBC, Prospects and Target Jobs, the chart below shows the employability skills that most employers want to see in prospective candidates. These are applicable whether you are a new graduate or already in employment.

If you do not feel confident in any of the areas listed above, it is advisable to look for something that will help you polish up your skillset. As well as that, have a think about what transferable skills you have. For instance, 'being able to plan activities and see them through' does not necessarily have to be in a workplace environment, the skill itself is transferable so if you have had similar experience, it is worth noting it.

There are probably quite a few ways in which you meet that requirement through the things you have done in other parts of your life. For instance, you may have organised a large social event or you may volunteer for a group that holds regular meetings and you make the arrangements for that. Thinking widely about your experience is a good way of being able to showcase your skills.

When you have completed the table with examples, go back up to the table at Activity 6.5 and see if you would still rate yourself at the same level having thought about the skills you have, but perhaps had not realised that you had. These transferable skills should provide you with examples that you can showcase on your CV and in your online profile.

Summary

Taking part in online courses means that you are likely to be involved in a number of academic-style discussions about its content as well as some more informal 'chats'. It is important to remember that you are in a professional situation with any number of people either with whom you already work, or with whom you may work in the future. If you are seeking to obtain a job, maybe find a new one, or even move forward in the one you already have, as a professional, every day is an interview! This applies no matter what online medium you are using, whether that is social media, training or networking sites.

It is entirely likely that you will come into contact with those same people again at some point in another online medium such as LinkedIn, another course, on social media of some description, in person at an interview, a conference or some other kind of face-to-face situation. The way you took part in the online course will have created an impression that may (or may not) be to your advantage when it comes to the 'real-life' situation.

Being able to meet and network with people that you would not otherwise have come into contact with is one of the greatest advantages of attending online courses and joining career progression sites such as LinkedIn. Both offer you the chance to present a much wider idea of who you are, as well as showcase your CV. So, you could say that these situations act as a preliminary interview and this is why it is so important to create and maintain the best online professional profile you can.

Key points from this chapter

- It is important to create a good impression when learning online and to be careful to use the relevant language and level of formality.
- Creating an online academic self is closely linked to your professional self.
- Whatever online sources are used, whether they are formal or informal, can have an impact on your job prospects and professional progression.

7 Researching Online

In this chapter you will learn about:

- the meaning of the term 'research'
- what makes a source 'academic'
- when to start researching for an assignment
- developing a timeline for research
- making use of a library catalogue
- deciding on useful search terms
- planning an internet search
- bookmarking internet pages so you can find them again
- how to judge the suitability of a website
- what research means within an academic context.

What is research?

Research simply means finding something out. It is something that most people do almost daily in some form or another. It might be that you want to know what is on at the cinema, or how much something costs. You could find this out by making a phone call, looking in the local press or by going online. To find out something online means entering specific search terms such as the name of your local cinema or shop into an online search engine.

Normally you will get more than one 'hit', which means that there will be several web pages for you to choose from and these may or may not contain the information that you are looking for. You might find out what you want to know on the first site that you look at, or you may look at several to get a range of detail concerning what you want to know.

You may end up spending time browsing through the pages that come up, clicking on links within them, and looking at a much wider range of things than you need or had originally intended to. This could be a good thing because you are able to gather lots of information that you had not thought about looking for, or it may end up being non-productive taking up valuable time.

When it comes to carrying out an academic search, you may choose to work with a combination of hard copy books and online sources. But if you do not have access to a brick university or college library, looking for sources online is a suitable alternative and a useful addition.

Doing online research to find ideas, examples and evidence for your assignments is basically the same as looking for anything else. You would use key words, but the sources you choose need to be academic in nature and closely related to the assignment topic. Even if there are brick university or college libraries near you, doing additional research online is important because it means that you have access to innumerably more sources than if you were to use only hard copies. The ideal situation would be to use a combination of the two, but this is not always possible.

What is an 'academic' source?

Making sure that the sources you use in your assignments are reliable is essential. It may be that you are being asked to write an essay, compile a report, do a book review or simply gather information in preparation for a class. Whatever the case, the information that you use needs to be the result of work done to a certain standard to ensure that the data it contains has been independently verified and peer reviewed.

Using material like this is one of the ways in which you can support what you are saying with confidence and helps to move those statements from being simply an opinion to being an academic argument. You will need to read widely to get a balanced view of the topic and to find information that you can then use either to create the argument by putting forward the conclusions of other scholars with the appropriate references, or to back up what you want to say showing that your view is based on evidence. Alternatively, you could use sources to argue against and create a new conclusion.

Examples of academic sources include:

Books: Books provide an extensive in-depth examination of a topic or subject. These are the result of extensive research by an author who will have undertaken rigorous checks to make sure that the information they present is correct. The assertions made will also be backed up by evidence that has been independently checked and verified by reviewers and editors. There will be references so that you can find and look at the evidence yourself to see how the author has reached their conclusion(s). Books contain a reference list/bibliography, contents page and index to help you navigate the subject matter.

Journal articles: These are not the same as articles found in the popular press such as magazines. Academic journals are produced by professional and scholarly publishers and provide a focused, in-depth discussion of a particular topic. They will be written by an expert in the field and contain original research findings, scholarly reports and point towards the methodology and theory behind the inquiry. They will also be peer reviewed.

Primary sources: A primary source might be a source that you are studying such as a piece of literature, an interview or piece of empirical data. They also include ancient literary sources. A primary source might also be a painting, a piece of architecture or archaeology. You will need to interpret the meaning of a primary source in its own context and in the wider sphere of your discipline so that you can talk about it in your assignment.

Creating a timeline

Almost any type of assignment, whether it is an essay, a report or an independent project, will require you to do some research. This is because you need to support what you are saying with evidence so that you present an academic argument and not just an opinion.

It is not always easy to know where to start, and what to look for, so before going online and looking for ideas or sources, you will need to do some planning. This is because there are endless sources of information online, both on search engines and in online library catalogues. So, depending on what your assignment or project is, how many words you are expected to write and how much time you have to work on it, there needs to be a set of parameters laid down to keep you on track.

The first one of these is time. Every assignment will have a deadline, so working out how much time you have from now until when it is due in is a good place to start. Some courses will have continuous assessment where assignments are due in at regular intervals, while others may only have one large assignment due at the end of the course.

Whichever applies to the course that you are taking, you will find that while the deadline may feel a long way off now, it will come around quicker than you think once you get started on the coursework. Therefore, putting the dates that assignments are due on a paper calendar in a prominent place can be a useful reminder.

The first thing to do is to check your assignment handbook or the assignments section of your Student Home Page to check when the assignment is due. From here, you can work backwards to create a timeline.

Research is only one part of the assignment writing process and cannot be done until you have a good understanding of the question. Spending time thinking about the key words in the question and looking at any guidance notes that you have been given is the starting point. Without really understanding what the question is asking and having a general idea of how you want to answer it, you cannot know what it is that you need to find out when it comes to doing your research.

Once you have completed Step 1, you should have a good understanding of what the question is asking. From here, you can start to work out how to answer the question and this will depend on the wordcount that has been allocated to it. For example, if your assignment can be no more than 600 words long, you will be able to make far fewer points than if it were 2,500 words, and obviously you will also need to do far less research in order to answer it. Once you have thought about this, you can start to look for both background information

Activity 7.1

Create a timeline for your assignment working backwards from the due date.

Today's date		Time for each step
Date that the assignment is due		
Step 1	Understanding the question and creating an initial plan	complete by	1 week
Step 2	Creating research questions and finding the answers	complete by	1 week
Step 3	Finalising your plan and collecting any extra resources	complete by	2 weeks
Step 4	Writing up the first draft and doing the first proofread and edit	complete by	2 weeks
Step 5	Finalising the assignment and checking references and style	complete by	1 week

and specific details to use in your answer. But before you start searching, it is important to consider where you will look to make sure that you get the best and most relevant content.

The general rule for assignments is that you use between 5% and 10% of the wordcount for the introduction, and the same for the conclusion. So if, for example, you were writing a 2,500 word assignment, this would use up to 500 words leaving only 2,000 to answer the question.

Given that each point made also needs to have evidence to back it up and some analysis to show how it helps to answer the question, there is likely to be room for only four or five main points.

If your assignment or project is shorter, you will have less and if it is longer, you will have more. The important thing is to stay within the remit of the exercise and be wary of over-researching. This is because if you have too many sources, you may end up wanting to use them all and this will mean that your work would be littered with examples with no room for analysis. This is one of the reasons why it is worth spending time on figuring out exactly what the question is asking and what the markers are expecting to see. The guidance notes for your assignment will probably point you towards the answers to these two things.

With a firm grasp of what the question is asking, you need to think about what you already know, and what you need to find out. Then you can start to design your research strategy.

Having a plan of how you are going to do your research is just as important as having an essay plan. It will mean that you do not waste valuable time on sources that are no use to you. A solid plan means that you use all the relevant search tools available and this will help to make sure that you do not miss anything that would work really well in your assignment.

The first thing you will need is background information. A general internet search might give you details of books or articles that you cannot get to because they are contained within a pay-only site. If they are academic journals or books though, you will probably be able to get to them free of charge through your university or college library, so this is a good place to start.

Using a library catalogue

It is likely that you will have been given access to the library belonging to your university or college as part of your course. The details of how to do this will be on your Student Home Page. Once you have located the link and accessed the library, you will be able to search different subject-specific lists, or search in general terms.

It is a good idea to start with the resources that are specifically for your subject as this will make it quicker and easier for you to find what you need. However, you can also search the main library catalogue using key words related to what you need to find out for your assignment.

Using the online library catalogue search engine, you can put in key search terms and books and articles that have one or more of those key words in the title will come up. It is worth bearing in mind that a library search cannot check the chapter headings or indexes of hard copy books, so you may miss out on finding a really useful source.

You should never underestimate the power of serendipity and if you are able to physically go to the library and browse the shelves, you may come across sources that you had not previously known existed.

For instance, if you are going to write about 'poverty in Victorian Britain', you could start by putting that complete phrase into the search bar. The first few results of what could be many thousands of hits, might look something like this:

Search term: poverty in Victorian Britain, Number of hits: 21,148

1 ARTICLE
The Emotions of Motherhood: Love, Culture, and Poverty in Victorian Britain
Griffin, Emma, The American historical review, 2018-02-01, Vol.123 (1), p.60–85

2 NEWSLETTER ARTICLES
Recent Findings from E. Griffin and Co-Authors Yields New Data on Social Science (The Emotions of Motherhood: Love, Culture, and Poverty In Victorian Britain)
Science Letter, 2019-03-08, p.1493–1493

3 ARTICLE
Adam Matthew released Poverty, Philanthropy and Social Conditions in Victorian Britain Information today, 2020-05-01, Vol.37 (4), p.29

4 ARTICLE
Poverty, Philanthropy and Social Conditions in Victorian Britain
Choice (Middletown), 2020-12-01, Vol.58 (4), p.350–350

5 REVIEW
Poverty and the Workhouse in Victorian Britain
Rose, Michael E., The English Historical Review, 1994-04-01, Vol.109 (431), p.491

6 REVIEW
Poverty and the Workhouse in Victorian Britain
Benson, John, History, 1992-10-01, Vol.77 (251), p.525-525

The selection above represents some of the more than 21,000 hits that came up. Some of what you see here are academic journal articles and some are reviews of articles or books. You will not know what is going to be useful to you without clicking on the hyperlinks which are included (usually underlined and in bold). However, you do not need to read the whole article to figure this out – you can just read the abstract, which is a summary at the beginning of the article, much like the blurb on the back on a book.

E-books will also be available in online libraries and with these, you will be able to look at the chapter headings and indexes before you decide to download them to see if they might be useful. You may be able to 'borrow' the whole book but the time that you can keep it for is likely to be restricted, often to just a few days.

Activity 7.2

Choose a topic to search for in the library catalogue of your university or college. Note down the search term(s) that you use and how many hits you get for each one. Try to narrow down the number with each new set of words you choose. If you find that the number of items that come up increases, go back and start again.

	Search term	Number of hits
1.		
2.		
3.		
4.		
5.		

Alternatively, you may be able to download PDF copies of some chapters, which you can store for use when you start writing. As with any source, you should make sure that you make a note of all the bibliographical details including the name of the author, the date of publication, the name of the publisher and city of publication and, of course, the page number(s) that you want to use. You will need this information for when you cite the source in the main body of your work and so that you can include it in your bibliography.

There is nothing worse storing a really good source but then when you come to use it, being unable to find the publication details. If this happens, you will not be able to include the source at all as you run the risk of plagiarism by being unable to produce a reliable reference for it.

Refining your search terms

When searching online for sources to use in your assignment either through an online search engine or when using a specific library catalogue or database, it is often difficult to narrow down the search terms enough to avoid getting too many hits. But creating a list of key words or phrases with a good idea of what you need to find out in order to answer the question is essential. Putting these key words into a search engine is likely to throw up hundreds, if not thousands, of hits, most of which will not be of any use to you. Therefore, the way in which you search needs to be strategic.

You can use your original list of key words and phrases to carry out a general sweep and, depending on what you find, then refine these search terms again to make sure that you can get to relevant information quickly and easily.

There are a number of ways of doing this (adapted from Spencer, 2021):

Search using multiple words: It is useful to start with multiple words because a one-word search query will not give you a targeted enough result. For example, searching for *Victorian workhouse numbers* rather than just *workhouse* will give you a smaller and more specific set of search results. Start with the shortest relevant search query, see what results you get, then refine it by adding either more, or fewer, words and operators after that if the results are too broad or narrow.

Case insensitivity: Searches are not usually sensitive to capitals when doing a general search. However, these are important when using the Boolean operator (see below).

Superfluous words: Overly common words like *the, an, of, in, where, who* and *is* are known as stop words. Online search engines usually omit these words from a query unless they are part of a common phrase, a name of a place, the title of a book, etc. You should also avoid putting a question into an internet search engine or library catalogue. An example of this might be, *How many children lived in poverty in Victorian Britain?* The extra words such as *how* and *many* will probably not appear in the documents or sources that you are looking for and this means that a large number of useful sources will be eliminated from your search.

Exact phrases: If you are looking for a phrase rather than a collection of words interspersed in the document, try putting inverted commas around your search query. This means that the search engine will match those words only if they occur within an exact phrase. Unless you put the phrase within inverted commas, the search will return sources where those words appear in any order, anywhere on the webpage or, if you are using a library catalogue, in the title of a book or in the main body of an article. This will increase the number of hits that you get exponentially.

Word order: It is important to consider the order of the words you use in your search query, because it can affect not only the number of results, but the relative rankings of those results as well. Sources in which those words or phrases appear in the order given in your search query will appear higher up in the list of results.

Singular versus plural: Think about whether what you are looking for is more likely to contain the singular or plural form of a given key word, and then use that form in your search query.

Wildcard: The asterisk acts as a wildcard character and allows you to omit one or more words in a search phrase. This is useful in a number of ways. If you are unsure of exactly what you are looking for, or how to phrase it, you can substitute a word or name that you cannot remember or which has multiple spellings. Note that asterisks can be used as a substitute only for an entire word and not for a part of a word.

Number range: Your search can span a wide numerical or date range and you can indicate the range by using two dots between two numbers or dates. For example, a search for data on Victorian poverty between 1850..1870 will find sources that mention any of the intervening years. As a shortcut, you can leave off the second date and simply put in Victorian poverty 1850.., which will match any date after that time. If you are looking for monetary terms, you could put in £20,000..£50,000 and this will give you matches anywhere within that range whether or not there are commas in the figures.

Punctuation: Other than these special characters (wildcard and range indicators), most punctuation within search terms is ignored. An important exception is the hyphen. A search query of on-site consulting will be interpreted as onsite consulting OR on-site consulting OR on site consulting. The hyphen indicates a strong relationship between two words; the underscore symbol also connects two words under most conditions. Another important exception is the apostrophe, which is matched exactly if contained within the word. For example, households will return different results from household's as one is a singular possessive and the other plural.

Accents: Accents are another exception. For search terms and phrases that include accents, always perform your search with and without the accent to ensure a complete set of results.

Boolean logic: You may find that you want to match on both the singular and plural forms of a word. In that case, you can use the OR search operator, as in Victorian children OR child. Note that the OR should be capitalized to distinguish it from 'or' as a key word.

Stemming: Sometimes search engines automatically match variations of a word. This is called stemming and it is done by matching words that are based on the same stem as the key word entered as a search term. You can disable the automatic stemming of a word by putting quotes around it.

Synonyms: You can expand your search beyond stemming to incorporate various synonyms which will increase the number of sources that come up.

Planning an internet search

There are a number of encyclopaedia style websites such as Wikipedia that will give you a lot of information on your subject. While sources such as these are very useful to give you a general idea about a topic, they are not acceptable as academic evidence and should never be cited in an assignment. However, they tend to contain some form of referencing with a list of sources at the bottom of the page, so if you find that there is an idea or a point that you think would be useful to you in your assignment, you should look at the original source and use that instead.

There are also many web pages that lead you to other non-academic sources and just because something is published on the web, it does not mean that it is accurate or even true. If you are in any doubt, it is best to consult your tutor for advice.

When you find a page that you think might be useful, you do not need to read the whole page to find your key words, you can search for those words by using Ctrl (or Command if you are using a Mac) and then F to open up the Find toolbar. Then you can enter the word or phrase that you are looking for and it will be highlighted for you. Also, as you search, it is a good idea to bookmark the sites that you think are going to be useful so that you can find them again. By clicking on the star on the search bar, you can give the bookmark a name and save it. You can do this in any browser.

Cloud-based bookmarking tools

If you are likely to be working on a different computer at any point, you should click on sync (usually found on the top right of the screen) to sync your devices. This means that you can sign into Google Chrome on any device and you will

Activity 7.3

Consider the most common types of web pages as listed below and consider whether or not you think that they are suitable sources of information for academic work.
(See Appendix 4 for the answers and some examples of each type of site.)

Blogs	A blog is a record of an individual's thought, opinions or experiences put online for others to read.	Y/N
Wikis	A wiki is a website that allows users to add, delete and edit the contents. As such it has multiple authors. The information is not always referenced.	Y/N
Q & A sites	Where named members of the public can ask questions which are answered by other individuals. Writers may or may not use their own names when contributing to these sites.	Y/N
Forums or groups	Open to anyone who joins the group. Discussions take place in threads and are often arranged on different pages with the question as the title. Contributors may or may not use their real name.	Y/N
Scholarly works	Peer-reviewed academic journal articles, e-books or scans of hard copy books which have a clearly stated author whose provenance can be traced.	Y/N
News articles	Using the electronic version of the print copy, which may draw content from a variety of sources. Generally, the author is identified.	Y/N
Databases and archives	A site that contains a large amount of information stored in a way that can be accessed easily. There will usually be additional details showing how to reference the information stored there.	Y/N
Documents	Any uploaded document in one file type or another. It may not be clear who has written the document or where the information that it contains comes from.	Y/N
Information pages	Pages providing information on a topic that may or may not have a clear author. These contain a great deal of information that is written in an accessible manner and is easily understood.	Y/N

Activity 7.4

Choose an internet source that you might want to use in your assignment. Check its provenance against the following criteria to see if it is reliable enough to use in an academic context. Firstly, note down all the details you can find about it.

Title of website	
Author	
Qualifications of the author	
Date written	
Publisher or owner of website	
URL	
Date accessed	

Now check whether the following information is available:

Authority	Who is the author, what can you find out about them and are contact details available? Have you heard of them elsewhere and have they written other things on this topic?
Affiliation	If you can find out who the owner of the website is, are they connected to a reputable institution or organisation such as a university or research lab? Educational sites usually have .edu or .ac, government sites might have .gov or .nhs at the end of their web address. Sites that end in .org are more difficult to trace and so should be treated with caution.
Audience	Who is the target audience for the site? You need to make sure that it is aimed at the same level as your course so that you avoid using sources that are too basic or too complex.
Date	Is the site up to date and can you find that date? A major site such as a museum or government page will be updated regularly, so you can be confident in using it. If you are using a report or data, be sure to check the date to make sure that it is current and has not been superseded. If it is more than a year old, you will need to find out if there is anything more up to date that you can use.

Reliability	Is the information factual as opposed to an individual's opinion? Are you able to verify the content elsewhere, preferably in a print document rather than being quoted elsewhere online? Check this in the library catalogue of your institution. Is the content free from bias and objectively presented and argued? Is the site well-presented and free from grammatical or spelling errors and other signs of sloppiness?

be able to access your bookmarks. However, it is inadvisable to sign into Chrome on a public computer because even after you have signed out, it may be possible for other people to access your data.

So, to be on the safe side, when you find a site that is of interest to you, you should bookmark it but also make a note of the URL and the date that you accessed the site in case you decide to use it in your work. Sometimes the content of sites changes, and your marker will need to be able see what it said on the date that you read it.

One way of making sure that you can always get to any sites that you have bookmarked is to use a cloud-based bookmarking tool.

Google Bookmarks: This is very useful as it means that you can access your bookmarked pages on whatever device you are using. This is a free service but you will need to have a Google account to use it.

Diigo: There are both free and paid for versions of this software. It allows you to bookmark sites, highlight parts of the page, add comments and send bookmarks to other people

Instapaper: This is a paid-for service that allows you to save articles, videos and pretty much anything else you find in your searches. You can add notes to the bookmarks and access them both on- and offline.

Once you have some good background information on your topic that supplements the course material, you can start to look for more specific sources that you can cite as evidence to back up what you are going to say in your assignment.

Checking the authenticity of online sources

When using any source in your assignment(s), you are responsible for checking the provenance, authenticity and accuracy of that source.

If you can find out this important background information and are happy with the answers to the questions you ask of it, then it is probably a useful source for you to use. The important thing is to approach sources that you find online with the same level of critique that you would a written source.

Summary

Researching online is different from traditional research using hard copy sources in a brick university or college library. The advantage it has over traditional research is the wealth of resources available to you, but it is not without its problems and must be used with caution.

The printed resources that you find online in an online library catalogue will have been subjected to a rigorous process called 'peer review' before they were published. This makes them reliable sources for you to use to inform your thinking, to cite and to build your academic argument around.

In contrast, sources on the internet may not have been subject to that process as anyone can upload just about anything. They must be treated with extreme caution as there is no set standard or method that is used to identify whether a source is true and reliable and the information it contains may not have been cross-referenced.

That is not to say that all internet sources are problematic. As long as you check the provenance of the author and the information that they are presenting, you should be able to use it. If you are in any doubt about the reliability of an internet source, check with your tutor who will be able to advise you.

Key points from this chapter

- Do not rely exclusively on internet sources. It is likely that your assignment will need resources found in a library, whether that is an online or brick library.
- Any source you find on the internet should be checked against information you find in a source from the library to make sure that it is reliable and authoritative.
- Before you start researching, decide on the key points you want to make in your assignment so that you know what you are looking for. The internet contains such a vast amount of information that you risk being overwhelmed and end up going off topic and spending far too much time trying to find your way around.
- Create key words or phrases that you can put into an internet search engine or the search box of an online library to speed things up.
- Spend some time finding out about the subject directories on your university or college library site and the scholarly internet sites that give you access to reliable peer-reviewed sources such as Google Scholar and Academia.edu.

- If possible, attend virtual library tours put on by your course provider to help you learn how to use the library and find out what type of internet sources are useful for your subject or discipline.
- Keep detailed records of all the information that you find, including the author, title, publisher and city of publication. If you use an internet source, make a note of the URL and the date you visited the site. All of this will be needed for your references and bibliography.
- To avoid mistakes, cut and paste the details into a document or referencing software.

8 Digital Technologies for Learning Online

By the end of this chapter you will:

- be able to use your Personal Learning Environment to support your own learning
- make effective use of your own hardware such as your printer, your webcam and storage
- understand the differences between Virtual and Managed Learning Environments
- appreciate how to access various online services such as forums, Twitter, Facebook, etc.

This chapter will help you understand the variety of digital technologies in the online learning arena and what they mean specifically to you as a learner. Additionally, it looks at how you can organise your use of the online tools available to help you avoid some of the pitfalls of learning online.

It is likely that you will encounter different kinds of learning environments during your studies and research, so knowing how they overlap and interact with each other can help to enhance your learning experience.

Your internet connection

A reliable and secure internet connection is a vital part of your Personal Learning Environment (PLE). Through your internet connection, you will be able to access the library, online databases, and any Virtual Learning Environment (VLE) or Managed Learning Environment (MLE) systems that your course provider offers. You will also be able to access online storage such as cloud services or a central file store if this is provided by your institution.

Most searchable online services and collections of journals, etc. will be accessible via the student credentials (username and password) provided to you by your college or university. Most educational establishments with a library will be able to help you access their services remotely through a system used by institutions across Europe called ATHENS.

If you are out and about, your internet connection could be via public internet services or network services provided by large external providers such as The Cloud, BT Wi-Fi, or smaller onsite networks provided by stores, restaurants and coffee shops. Some broadband suppliers give you free access to public Wi-Fi networks as part of their deal, so it is worth checking with your service provider. The important thing is to always make sure that any connection provided to you by external services is safe and secure. For more on this, see Chapter 10, *Troubleshooting, Staying Safe Online*.

Your internet connection needs to be easily accessible. It also needs to be reliable. Without your internet connection you will still be able to study if you have downloaded the course material or have paper copies, but you would not be able to do any research or discover anything new that is not already stored on your computer or in your files. Without access to the internet you would still be able to type-up assignments, but you would not be able to submit anything electronically or send email. All of this should be factored into your choice of internet service provider and any public services you use.

Pay attention to the small print on any agreement you might enter into with a service provider, particularly looking to see if there are any guarantees of service availability. You need to know what would happen if they cannot provide what they say they will. A suitable example is the promise from some telecoms companies that they will provide alternative access through a portable wireless 4G/5G hub if their main service fails, and this will be delivered within an agreed time.

It is well worth having a plan for how you would study if your internet provider lets you down. You may be able to access the internet through your mobile phone and connect your computer or tablet via a hot spot but this may incur data charges and may be slow.

Activity 8.1

Think about what you would do if you lost your fixed internet connection for more than 24 hours. Make an action plan taking into consideration the following points:

What will your service provider do to help if there is a problem and how long will this take? Is there an interim solution that they can offer?	
Is mobile data via your phone viable? Will it be part of your data plan or will it cost you more money? Is it fast enough?	
Would public Wi-Fi – at a library, shopping centre, etc. – work for you in terms of your learning needs?	

Your digital resources

The digital resources start with the devices that you use to access the internet. This might be a desktop or laptop computer, a phone, a tablet, or some combination of these. You may have more than one of each type of device, and you may have a local file server in your home for the purposes of sharing printers and storage of your computer files.

Ideally, the devices you choose should be compatible with each other, particularly in the case of whatever word processing application you use so that you can swap between them. Most devices will allow you to work and save in Microsoft Word format or similar, but do check that you can open the files when moving between devices so that you do not lose key features such as formatting and typeface. Ensure that whatever choice you make is compatible with the requirements of your course.

Your laptop or tablet should be robust, in that it should be easily connected to your internet, however you might normally do so without frequently losing the connection and having to type in your details each time. If these are battery powered, they should be capable of working for some considerable time before requiring recharging, or able to charge and run while connected to the mains electricity supply.

Your devices should have reasonable storage capacity so that you can store downloads of core texts, course materials and personal files. In the case of computers, this is likely to be the fixed hard disk inside; smaller devices such as tablets do have internal storage in the form of memory.

You should avoid having only one form of storage. You can use cloud storage to keep your contents safe such as OneDrive, Dropbox and Google Drive among other similar systems, as long as you have taken suitable precautions to protect your access. You can make copies onto removable storage such as portable hard drives and USB sticks.

The important thing is not to rely on just one method. Each has risks, electronics can fail, and 'finger trouble' such as accidental deletions can happen, so the more 'safe methods' of storage you have, the less likely it is that you might permanently lose any vital data.

Secure passwords, known only to you, help to keep your devices secure (see Chapter 10, *Troubleshooting, Staying Safe Online*, for advice on passwords).

Backing up and restoring

If you are moving between devices or do not have a fixed backup system, cloud storage or external storage device, you may consider using your email to store copies of your current files. To do this, email a copy to yourself and it will be stored in your 'sent mail' folder within your email service and should appear also in your inbox.

You may wish to email it to a family member or trusted friend. This may not be a viable option if your files are quite large because most email systems will not allow file attachments bigger than 25Mb in size. There may also be a limit to the amount of storage you can have in your sent and received emails as many providers will not allow storage of more than 5Gb of mail. If you exceed this, you may not be able receive any more email until you reduce the amount of storage you are using. To get around this, you could zip your files and only save them once, either in your sent or received mail.

> **Activity 8.2**
>
> Test your backup and restore process.
>
> | | |
> |---|---|
> | Where will you copy your files to? | |
> | Can you access the files directly from where you have copied them? For example, from your memory stick, hard disk or cloud. | |
> | Copy your files back, taking care not to overwrite the ones you are currently working on. Do they open with no problems? | |
> | If your memory stick or external hard drive does not work, what will you do to reduce the risk of losing your files? | |
>
> **N.B. Check and test your backup/restore process regularly to be sure that it works**

Filing and retrieving your work

Consider how you will structure the storage of your digital resources and files. If you were using a physical filing cabinet, you would have different drawers for different things. Within these drawers you would have dips to put things in, and within these dips you would store individual pages either directly or in folders. Each drawer, dip and folder would be named, colour coded or numbered so that you would know what was in them and how to find them. You might have them arranged alphabetically or by date.

You can structure your digital data in a very similar way as file and folder names often have a 255-letter limit, so you can be quite descriptive if need be. This naming of your data is very important so that you can find it again. If you are unable to find it, for instance if it is not where you expect it to be, if you have given it a clear file name, you should be able to locate it through a key word search.

As you work, you should save as you go. If you are making a lot of edits, it may be useful not to overwrite what you have done, but to save the different version under a new name such as Essay 2 v.1, Essay 2 v.2, etc. Another reason for doing this is that you might later decide to use something that you cut and if you save your work as separate versions, you will be able to go back in and find it. If everything has the same name, there is always the risk that you might copy an older version of your work over the top of your latest complete version, which will cost you time and effort in re-writing it.

One such suggested convention is:

MyDocument-Version-DRAFTorFINAL-Date-Any-extra-notes-My-Name.Doc

For example:

Dissertation-V3-DRAFT-31-January-2022-With-Title-Page-and-Finished-Appendices-J-Jones.Doc

It seems long, but it comprises just 79 characters – remember your limit is 255 – and it clearly shows you what should be in the document. It is Version 3 of your Dissertation, you are still working on it as it is a draft, the last date you worked on it was the end of January and you have included the final version of your appendices and a title page.

Some institutions prefer for your name to be included. Sometimes they ask for your student number or module code too, so be sure you know what your course provider wants.

Naming your files clearly provides clarity and takes the guess work out of finding your data.

Activity 8.3

Consider your current filing system for your information. Use this checklist to make sure that it is right for you.

Do you have one?	
How does it work?	
How easy is it to file things and find them again?	
How do you know how to find things? Do you use an index? Folders? Alphabetical order?	
Can you find a specific piece of information that you have already stored without having to read it through to know you have chosen the right one?	

Safeguarding your work and data

The concept of using cloud storage, removable memory sticks and making copies has already been touched upon, however, it cannot be emphasised enough that you should back up your important files. Most computer operating systems have a facility to copy, back up and/or restore data. There is not much point in making copies if you have no mechanism for restoring the information when you need it, it has to be a two-way process.

Apple has an application called Time Machine, which allows it to create a backup of part or all of its internal hard drive. Microsoft Windows has legacy programs called 'Backup' and 'Restore', which are based on older Windows technology, but still provided with current versions of Windows. These complete or automated backups are useful and effective; however, you need to consider what will work best for you.

First consider the operating system and applications that you use when studying. Did your computer come with the ability to re-install itself from scratch if there was a problem? Your computer may have been shipped with a DVD copy of the operating system, or it may have come with it all pre-installed and an electronic backup already on the computer ready to use. But can you activate it?

The computer will have had an instruction sheet when you took it out of the box explaining how to do this. It might be that your computer is second hand or was given to you, and this information was not provided. If you no longer have the instructions, you will be able to find the details online.

Your applications, i.e. the programs that you use, should not be a problem. If they were legitimately obtained and you have a valid licence you might still have the original packaging, or at least a downloaded copy with a valid licence key stored on your computer.

You should ensure that this information is kept safe, and that you have a copy of any downloaded software you rely on with the appropriate licence key stored on some removable media like a USB memory stick or external hard drive. This will ensure that if you lose the program you can re-install it from scratch. However, this will not protect your data files.

For your computer's operating system, e.g. Windows or MacOS, if you do not have the original media the software was shipped on or you do not have a recovery tool, your first port of call should be where you bought it from. Failing that, consult the computer manufacturer's website where you will see a 'Support' or 'Technical' option on the menu. You ought to be able to search for the answer. In the worst case scenario, you may need to buy a new copy of the operating system and a valid licence to re-install it.

It is always worth asking your learning provider if they supply students with any kind of discount on system software. Using this will give you access to updates and a port of call if you need help to re-install it for any reason.

Miscellaneous devices and hardware

Using the various applications and services on the internet, particularly engaging with group and face-to-face video systems and similar technologies, will require the ability to send video from a camera mounted in your computer or on/beside it, called a webcam. In addition to the webcam, you may have other 'peripherals' attached to your computer such as a printer, a scanner, or a stylus and tablet.

It is vitally important to make sure all these are working in advance of tutorials to avoid being in the situation of five minutes before your first face-to-face synchronous (in real time) online seminar, you realise that you do not have a working webcam, or that you do not know how to turn on the computer's microphone.

Build yourself a mini checklist along the lines of the table below in order to ensure that you understand each device and know how to use it.

Activity 8.4

Checklist. Make sure you know the answers to all these questions so that you can avoid any last minute problems with printing documents or connecting to a live session.

Printer	
Do you need a printer for your study? Online courses usually ask for assignments to be submitted electronically. However, it can be useful to have a printer if you prefer reading on paper than on the screen.	
What kind of printer is it? Is it inkjet, or a laser? Is it colour or black and white?	
Do you have spare ink cartridges? Replacement cartridges can be expensive and so this should be factored in when choosing which printer to buy. Sometimes the printers that are a little more expensive have refillable cartridges which works out much cheaper in the long run.	
What paper do you need? For example, A4, A3, card, plain, photo paper?	
How is your printer connected to your computer, phone or tablet? Is it by a USB cable? Wi-Fi? Bluetooth?	

Do a test print of both colour (if your printer has colour ink) and black and white. Does your printout look as you expected it?	
If you need to print documents and do not have a printer, where else might you be able to do this? What is the cost of doing this?	
Webcam	
What kind of webcam is it? What is the resolution and is it high definition? Does it have a built-in microphone?	
How is it attached? Is it built into your desktop or laptop or do you have to connect it via a USB cable?	
Can you tell when it is transmitting images? It should have a small LED light showing that it is active like on a laptop. This is very important for your privacy.	
Does it work with all your software or apps? In software like Skype and Zoom there is a 'set up your audio/video' menu option to confirm that it is working – test this to see.	
Can you mute the video or blank it when you step away from the session? Is there an option on your camera or software to turn the video off while you remain connected to a live lecture or tutorial?	
Do you need a headset with a built-in microphone? If you hear echoes or distorted sound from using your computer's inbuilt microphone and speakers, you will need to get a headset. Earphones provided with a mobile phone can often work well if the plug is compatible with the ports in your computer or tablet.	

Microphones and headsets

The box above mentions using a headset for sound and a microphone. For privacy and clarity of sound if you are not at home or in a quiet space, it would be better to use a headset. No one will be able to hear what you are hearing, and the risk of a microphone picking up ambient sounds, cars passing in the street and unwanted audio distractions is much lower.

With open microphones like the ones built into most desktops and laptops, there is a risk that it will pick up the sounds coming out of your speakers and so set up a feedback loop which will increase in volume and distortion. Using a headset is the best way to avoid this.

Headsets come in two primary forms: one with jack plugs which are little single 2.5mm prongs you insert into your sockets for your 'speaker out' and 'microphone in' connections, or a single USB connection. For ease of use, USB connected headsets are simplest as you can usually just plug it in and it will sort itself out, as most of the USB technology is 'plug and play'. However, if your headset has the two jack connectors, they will most likely be colour-coded – green for your headphones and pink for your microphone. The sockets on your computer or tablet should also be obviously labelled with a miniature headphone symbol or a miniature microphone symbol.

If you do get them the wrong way round, you will not damage your equipment, but you will not hear anything through the headset. Reverse the connectors and you should hear the sound coming through as expected. To check this, if you have loaded an application that makes sounds or accessed a web page that plays back video/sound then you should see a small speaker icon on your computer's toolbar, on the bottom right for Windows-based computers. Click on this and you should be able raise or lower the volume which will be reflected in the sound you hear. If there is a line through it, the sound is muted. Unmute it by clicking on it or changing the volume and you should hear sound.

Virtual Learning Environments

Beyond your Personal Learning Environment (PLE), you will be interacting with material provided by your course of study. You will log on to institutional Virtual Learning Environment (VLE) systems using your web browser with credentials initially provided by your learning institution. Your institution may refer to these systems with their product names, such as Canvas, BlackBoard, WebCT, Moodle and others, sometimes customised by your institution.

These systems are all VLEs designed to provide the primary learning support for your course. For instance, you may find that pre-lecture or seminar reading material is posted there for you to see prior to the session being physically delivered. Your VLE may offer you a forum in which you can discuss your module or a lecture or seminar with other participants, all within the safe confines of your course of study.

Your VLE is not a replacement for teaching but is designed to supplement it and offer a way to enhance learning with links and storage of useful digital resources. It can provide links to video-based solutions within the structure of the VLE in order to deliver teaching live as well as links to recorded content that you can access offline. This is particularly useful for overseas students in different time zones and for people who are unavailable at the time the lecture is originally broadcast.

It should be stressed that the ideal is to attend the live version of the teaching to get the best from it. Personal interaction and the ability to ask questions in real time can go a long way towards understanding course material.

VLEs have other features such as the addition of assessment through built-in or 'plug-in' tools such as Questionmark Perception, allowing for the inclusion of a variety of secure and flexible question features from multiple choice, short answer and essay type responses.

Some VLEs interface with industry standard plagiarism checking systems such as Turnitin, within which you upload your work and it is automatically checked for plagiarism. It checks for duplication, copied content or similar phrasing when compared to its enormous database of referenced works, and a report is generated showing exactly how original your work is and highlighting any 'problem' areas.

VLEs can be also interfaced with other systems on campus to allow a personalised portal for your learning environment. This could include email integration, the ability to access your own student records, make payments, etc.

This wider integrated access is called a Managed Learning Environment (MLE), although the terms have started to become interchangeable with the focus being on the VLE/MLE as a resource and used as part of the individual's Personal Learning Environment. With all institutional VLE/MLE systems and

Activity 8.5

Consider your learning institution's services supporting your online learning

	Y/N
Does it have a VLE/MLE?	
What is it called?	
Can you log in and find your course materials?	
Can you see how to get help if you are unable to log in, or cannot find what you are looking for?	

If you cannot find the answers to any of these questions, contact the Computing Helpdesk of your institution. If you cannot find the number for this, call the main switchboard and ask to be put through.

their integrated services such as library access, student user guides will also be available for perusal and download. Your institution will have a helpdesk which you should be able to access by phone, email and forum or their online chat box. It is worth making a note of these details in case you cannot get into your student portal to access them for any reason.

The Student Support Team at your chosen institution will be happy to answer any questions, and you should feel free to share your question and the response you receive with your classmates. It is very likely that if there is something that you did not understand or cannot access, you will not be the only one!

Beyond your Virtual Learning Environment

Other services you may access include social media like Facebook and Twitter. Some are more useful than others in an educational context (see Chapter 9, *Using Social Media for Learning Online*), but as the face-to-face student experience embraces interaction and discourse with your peers, for online learning, social media may be a useful online equivalent.

It may well be that you already have existing social media accounts. If that is the case, you will need to be sure that whatever you do on social media is safe from a security, identity and health perspective.

It is up to you, but consider your social media presence and what exactly you want to engage in. You may find that the majority of your friends and/or classmates already use some technologies to communicate among themselves such as Instagram, SnapChat, WhatsApp, Facebook Messenger or text messaging. Make your choice based on what you want to get out of it as each system has pros and cons.

Facebook

Pros:

- Works on most platforms including phones, tablets, laptops, Macs and PCs.
- Very easy to use.
- Allows you to connect to people you know and makes suggestions of other people you might know.
- Easy to remove or edit your posts.
- It is likely that you or people you know will have already used Facebook. It has over 2.9 billion monthly active users (Zephoria, 2021).

Cons:

- Security concerns – Facebook has been hacked in the past and personal information including email, passwords and phone numbers have been resold on the 'dark net'.
- Very easy to make a mistake and post something inadvertently.

- Often suggests friends of friends and anyone with similar personal information such as your school, college, university, your employment history, and interests or clubs.

Twitter

Pros:

- Works on most platforms including phones, tablets, laptops, Macs and PCs.
- Very easy to use and to reach individuals or groups of people interested in specific things.
- Automatic recommendation of 'trending' tweets.
- Easy to delete your tweets.
- Easy to block other users.
- It is possible that you or people you know will have already used Twitter. It has over 396.5 million active monthly users (DataReportal, 2021).

Cons:

- Very easy to make a mistake and tweet it.
- Limited size of posting to 280 characters.
- Limitations in size have given rise to a particular usage netiquette and other users can be intolerant of deviation.
- While you can delete your original post, it will not necessarily erase all memory of it and people can still comment.
- The subject markers, the '#' (hash tags) are not fixed and can be made up as you go. For example, #ThatsANuisanceHowWillIFindIt.

There are many other social media systems offering a plethora of content: Instagram with its pictorial postings; Snapchat with its short-lived snaps as postings; and LinkedIn, the job-related site for professionals 'linking up'. Two of the largest platforms, Facebook and Twitter, will be looked at more closely in Chapter 9, *Using Social Media for Learning Online*.

Educational support software

There are many applications and support packages that can help you study. The Student Support Team at your institution will be able to advise which one(s) are best for you. A good place to start is for you to think about what you need to be able to do – then see if you have the tools to do it.

First, you have to identify the need. The assumption is that you have your computer, laptop or tablet and you already have your web browser and your word processor, but you may need more software to address a particular need that you have. For instance, if you are writing a piece using a modern European language and you need software to enhance your understanding and vocabulary, is there a suitable application available for you? Many options exist including *Babbel*, *Rosetta Stone* and *Duolingo*.

Sometimes you may be struggling with an aspect of your study but have not considered that there might be some software to help you (see Chapter 5, *Recognising Strengths and Overcoming Difficulties and Disabilities*, for more advice on this). You can also contact your institution's Learning Support Team to discuss the problem and they will be able to help you define what your need actually is and suggest solutions.

Next, consider your need and what you would want any software to do to address your problem or enhance your learning. Bear in mind that some courses require or recommend particular supporting software and will provide you with a link to where you can get it, for example specific statistical analysis software, or drawing/Computer Aided Design (CAD) packages.

Your institution will probably have recommendations and may have a deal already in place that will allow you to use an app under their licence or at reduced or even at no cost to you. Be sure to check that it is compatible with your computer and the output from the software is usable with your other applications.

A good example is the iPad Notes app. It is very easy to type into, it has a workable voice interface if you want to dictate, and it is built into iPads and iPhones. The data stored in it, however, is not compatible with any word processor, but it does support 'cut and paste' on your phone or tablet and can be exported by email or text. Consider if this kind of integration is good enough to meet your needs.

It is also a good idea to read reviews. Use your web browser and search engine of choice to investigate your chosen solution. You may find that there are both positive and negative experiences of the package, but as with all things on the internet, closely consider the source of the information, making sure that it is reputable.

Speak to your friends and fellow students as they may have already solved the problem and can pass on what they learned.

Once you have the product installed, use it for a while, and then ask yourself the question: does it do what I need? If you find that it is difficult to use, or you are unsure about how to make it work well for you, ask for help. The Computer Help Desk or Student Support Team at your institution may have training materials that will solve the problem or make a recommendation about other sources of help.

The important thing is for you to be able to carry out your studies without having to struggle with the technology. If the software does not do everything that you need it to, do not waste your time and possibly your money. If it does not add anything to your experience and you find you are working round the software, rather than the software facilitating your work, then maybe it is not the right package for you.

Whatever technology you use should enable you, not disable you.

Summary

While you study online, your environment and tools used must facilitate your learning rather than impede it. Think about your resources and be sure that you can use them and know what to do if things do not quite go to plan, so you can cope with disasters ranging from losing your work to running out of printer ink when you are preparing your assignments. Remember, preparation and practice will help you use your PLE and your digital resources, so do not worry if it does not all fall into place straight away.

Key points from this chapter

- Build your PLE and make it work for you.
- Have a filing system and data store that you understand and where you can find anything you need quickly and easily.
- Make sure you know how to use your digital resources.
- Engage with the VLE/MLE provided by your institution.
- Look after yourself and your data.
- Choose software and tools that facilitate your work and make your learning broader and easier.

9 Using Social Media for Learning Online

By the end of this chapter you will be able to:

- evaluate the usefulness of different social media platforms in terms of how they can support your learning
- engage with social media platforms of your choice
- be aware of the risks of using social media and how to keep yourself safe
- use social media to your advantage while studying
- protect yourself and your online identity when interacting with others online.

Blogging

As the World Wide Web developed, blog sites appeared for individuals to have their say and project themselves out into the internet. A *blog* is a website that contains the thoughts and opinions of an individual user, usually in the form of a journal or commentary on whatever they have in mind. Things like videos, images and text might be posted, and the subject matter can be literally anything.

Some bloggers specialise in specific subject areas which might be helpful for your studies. For instance, there are a number of movie critic bloggers who write about the latest releases in cinema and give their own electronic thumbs up or down to the production. Others write about books they have read or talk about the development of a project such as an archaeological dig. Sometimes the departments of educational institutions have their own blogs.

Blogging has become a form of journalism for non-journalists and, in some instances, it has become successful to a point where it begins to challenge the established news outlets. However, unlike established news outlets with their legal departments and editorial oversight, some blogs can be controversial, apocryphal or just plain made up.

From a learning perspective, the most important factor in choosing a blog relating to a specialist subject relevant to your study, is to consider the reputation and qualifications of the blogger. The content of a blog may not be a suitable academic source in your chosen discipline, so be sure to check this with your course leader before including it in your assignments. Even if you cannot include the content, blogs can be useful in informing and expanding your thinking, giving you new ideas to think about.

Microblogging

Microblogging is similar to blogging but as its name suggests, the posts are shorter. With a blog, the posting is liable to be a complete piece or article; however, with microblogging, the initial post is more likely to be a short conversation starter and part of a larger system rather than a single blog site. For example, Facebook, Twitter, Instagram and to an extent the accompanying text with the posted photos on Instagram and the videos on YouTube and TikTok are perfect examples of such microblogging. Short posts are linked to the original by a thread. These types of micro-posts lend themselves to multiple reactive postings in response to the original, creating an ongoing conversation about it.

This ability to include multiple inputs and multiple replies adds to peer-type academic discussion. However, it must be remembered that these are likely to be open to anyone to comment on. Therefore, closed forums that exist within your own course site are likely to be more effective in communicating academic concepts. But microblogging, while sometimes more of a free for all, can often produce useful debate and food for thought.

Vlogging

Vlogging, or video blogging, is where the content is video based. Responses to posted videos can be in the form of a rating, commenting in text form, or posting video responses.

Like blogs and microblogs, the content can be varied, and the videos can be very short such as a TikTok 30-second viral video. But usually vlogging tends to be focused on specific subjects. YouTube, the video sharing system, is a useful place to look for information as it offers longer videos such as academic lectures or demonstrations. It also contains instructional videos on topics as diverse as how to play a board game to how to plaster a wall.

Choosing a vlogger to follow offers the same benefits and pitfalls as blogs and microblogs. There is such a wide range of content available from many different people and institutions that it is vital to consider the source and usefulness of the content carefully. If you are unsure, check with your tutor. Remember any direct information, or even ideas, that you take for use in your assignments must be referenced with the same stringency as other written or online sources.

Image sharing

Image sharing via social media is generally used for personal purposes, personal promotion or social influencing and so may well be of limited academic value. However, use the search tools that Pinterest and Instagram provide and consider the results. They may be of varying use to you as a student depending on what you are studying.

The rise and rise of Facebook

Facebook is the biggest of the social media systems in terms of active users. It was started by two students in an American college in 2004 and since then has grown into the multi-billion user and multi-billion-dollar fact of life that it is today. While its original intent was not for educational purposes, it is now widely used by educational institutions, businesses and individual users alike.

Discussion and debate are vital academic tools in formulating ideas and developing concepts in education, and much like open discussion in seminars, Facebook allows for unrestricted discussion up to a point. It has rules on participation and standards of posting which are policed by means of automatic detection systems and by a feedback system where users can complain about postings. As well as this, there will be a moderator keeping an eye on the content and comments on a particular site and they have the ability to remove posts that breach netiquette and other self-imposed rules. For personal sites, this will be the site owner who may have different ideas of what is suitable compared to those of an academic institution.

Academic discussion benefits from diverse viewpoints and to avoid missing crucial points and counter arguments in serious discussions, it is useful to subscribe to suitable groups so that you can be kept up to date with what is being said there through notifications into your own Facebook page.

Facebook also has a messaging tool, often referred to as a PM or personal message, for private discussion that is not visible to others. Although you send a message in this private way, it is important to be aware that the recipient may not keep your discussion private in the same way that a face-to-face discussion may not remain private.

The messenger capability is built into the web application, so if you are using Facebook on a desktop or laptop computer, it will automatically be there. However, if you are using a tablet or smartphone, *Messenger* is a separate app which will need to be installed.

If there is not a Facebook group for your course, it is worth thinking about creating one, being sure to put appropriate privacy settings in place. You might choose, for instance, to keep it a closed group, visible only to members of your tutor group, or you might want to make it a wider platform and allow past, current and prospective students of the course to join. It is worth doing a search, talking to others on your course and checking with your university or college department in advance to see if there is one already in existence that you can join.

When setting up a group, you will also have the responsibility of moderating it and putting into place the usual rules about netiquette that will make it clear to users what is, and is not, appropriate. You can do this via an initial post that you can pin at the top of discussions to keep it in view.

Fellow group users should be aware that you will remove anything that is inappropriate. This should include detailed discussions of assignments except in the case of group working, mark sharing and comments about tutors.

You can populate the group with details of your course and pass the name onto fellow students via the group forums or other communication tools built into your course. Take care in naming the group so that there is no ambiguity and so that others in your learning community can find it easily.

The kind of material you can post is quite diverse and can be in the form of simple text or images in various forms and also video content. You can include web addresses to highlight specific web pages on a website and can include postings from other social media platforms such as Twitter that you think are relevant and useful for your course. This will encourage academic discussion and provide a place for students to talk in an informal way, supporting each other practically and emotionally during their academic journey.

Having a group page like this is also useful if you are not comfortable in taking part in wider discussions because you can respond positively to a post with a simple click on the 'like' icon to demonstrate your support and agreement. Privacy of posting is shown by a small icon next to the original post. It also applies to photos and other media posts.

Consider the following:

- If you see a little globe depicting the earth next to the original post, this post is available to everyone on Facebook to see.
- If you see an image of two heads beside each other, this means that the original post was intended for the original poster's friends only.
- A group of three or more heads together denotes a posting that has group privileges. This means that any member of the group in which the original post was placed can see the contents.

In keeping with the earlier discussion in Chapter 2 of this book about *Online Identity and Personas*, you should note that creating a fake identity profile and appearing to be someone else is forbidden and the creator may be liable to having their access to Facebook removed. Depending on what is posted in someone else's name, legal action may be taken by the system owners and the individual being impersonated. Posts should be accurate and true. Remember that saying something on social media is the same as saying something in person and is *permanently* memorialised.

There are extensive Terms of Service for using Facebook and other social media sites, so remember that when you create your account you are agreeing to abide by these T&Cs so you should take care to read them (Facebook, 2021).

Twitter and tweeting

Twitter is a microblogging type system that has its roots in SMS text messaging, which is a simple messaging system also known as mobile phone text messaging.

Twitter is different to Facebook in one key way which is that your postings are all inherently global by default. Everything you post is visible to all other Twitter users worldwide and it is not possible to limit who sees what you post to a restricted list of friends as you can in Facebook.

While Facebook generates a tailored newsfeed for you using an algorithm based on your activity, and that of the users of any group of which you are a member, Twitter also provides you with a newsfeed based on the choices you have made and the posts you read. This can be a really useful tool for students because it means that you can 'follow' academics in your field of study keeping up to date with the latest discoveries, discussions and ideas in your discipline. You can also see details of who they themselves follow, and in turn who follows them.

Using Twitter is an easy way of finding out who some of the leading academics in your chosen discipline are. More than this, you will be able take part in those discussions which will inform your thinking and help you become part of the wider academic community.

If you are intending an academic career, bringing yourself to the attention of others in your field can be very useful. Remember though, what happens online spills over into real life, so being honest about your identity and the scope of your knowledge is very important.

There is a particular terminology surrounding Twitter:

Twitter term	Meaning
Tweet	A microblog posting to Twitter
Retweet	Resending or forwarding on with or without comment on someone else's tweet.
Twitter handle	The Twitter account name preceded with the @ symbol.
Twittersphere	The world of Twitter users.
Hashtag #	A designator for categorising a subject or concept posted to Twitter.
DM	A 'Direct Message' sent privately from one Twitter user to another.

Users on the system have an @, also known as the *at symbol*, preceding their Twitter account names. You should be familiar with the symbol as it is used in email communications to designate the destination of the mail. In Twitter it is used as follows:

@AccountName

Note, however, that the Twitter handle and the posting name can be different. If you create a Twitter account yourself, you might find that there is already someone on the system with the same or similar name to yours, and the *handle* (name) is already taken.

There is no specific rule that says your Twitter handle must resemble your own name, so handles can be extremely varied. If you want to make sure that someone sees your tweet, you can include their Twitter handle in your tweet. For example, you might put in the names of other students that you know, or your university, college or work handle.

Twitter also has the facility to send a private message to another user but this will depend on their privacy settings. Some people or institutions disable this facility in the same way that you yourself can.

Another key difference to other social media systems is in the way that posts can be put into categories. This is done by putting a hashtag in front of a term. For example:

#Education

These hashtags are searchable and when they are used by a lot of people they 'trend', which means that a lot of people have either retweeted the post or clicked on the 'like' symbol. You can use a hashtag to categorise your own tweets using whatever term you want. However, bear in mind that it may get you better exposure and a better response if you use existing appropriate hashtags – for example,

#LearningOnline or #onlinelearning,

which gives a good indication of what the discussion is about. Tweets can contain a variety of content, but posts are limited in length to 280 characters and you are able to add images and video clips but these are also limited according to size.

From a learning perspective, Twitter offers an element of signposting for your research. A tweet can include references to externally held material, and so the opportunity is there for tutors and peers to point out useful sources related to your discipline. Additionally, with the ability to include hashtags and Twitter 'handles' within the structure of the tweet, it is easy to include categories to consider and to bring others into the discussion.

> Example tweet
> @YourPeer Found this interesting article in the library – I found it earlier while researching the essay http://www.library.edu/madeup/article #UsefulResearch

The tweet above shows the inclusion of one of your peers and an external web address to look at and comment upon. But even though you have only included the name of one of your peers, what you have said is not private. Everyone that follows you will be made aware of the tweet, and it will be visible to anyone else who cares to look at your feed. Additionally, anyone following the hashtag, for example, *#UsefulResearch*, will also see it. Let us assume your peer replied.

Example Reply from @YourPeer to @You
Yes Might be worth checking with @YourLecturer to see if it's useful

Replies such as this are visible under the original tweet, creating a conversation thread. The publicly viewable text of the reply tweet does not include your Twitter handle but as it is in reply to your original tweet, you will automatically be alerted. The reply has included another Twitter user for their review, this time your lecturer. Again, let us assume your lecturer replied.

Example of a further reply from @YourLecturer
@You and @YourPeer Yes this is useful. It might be worth your while having a chat with @AnotherLecturer as that's her specialist area #UsefulResearch. Consider also #AlternativeResearch

As can be seen with this further reply to your original tweet, your lecturer has contributed an opinion and pointed both you and your peer towards another academic who specialises in your field of work, and through the use of hashtags has suggested that you consider an additional source.

While Twitter is not a primary or secondary source of information, it is a useful place to have a discussion and be pointed towards information sources that you can then follow up.

Establishing communication with your peers, tutors and others via social media

The main social media networks provide you with a search tool which, if not immediately obvious, can be found by using the magnifying glass icon. This will allow you to search for people you know or topics you are interested in.

The real trick is connecting with people that you might know, or know about, who have similar academic or social interests that could be informative, or useful, to you. On Twitter you can search for a particular topic through a hashtag such as Subject#. On Facebook you can search for a group name, or simply the name or email address of the person or institution you want to find.

Once you have an account on Facebook or Twitter, the systems will make recommendations of people for you to follow or send a friend request to. Facebook will also make suggestions of groups you may wish to follow based on your activity and that of contacts in your friends list. Twitter recommends trending hashtags based on overall traffic with some referral to people you follow.

The Twitter handle for the UK Prime Minister is not his name, but @10DowningStreet, and the Open University Twitter account is @OpenUniversity but this relates to the institution as a whole. There are more specific names for the various departments and disciplines that are worth following up on so that you can find out what is happening within your own learning community.

Activity 9.1

Consider the following points:

What social media platform(s) do you currently use?	
What do you think will be most useful to you? Consider this in terms of your own study. How does it support your learning or research?	
Do the features of the system allow for group work? How would you go about coordinating a collaborative project?	

Activity 9.2

Create an account on the social media platform(s) of your choice.

	Notes
Familiarise yourself with the web-based interface via a computer. If you have a tablet and/or smartphone, compare it with the mobile version of the application.	
Contact your peers via the respective messaging tools incorporated in the specific applications and establish a group.	

Your identity on social media

Social media is a two-way street. When creating your social media presence, it is important to consider how you present yourself online for a variety of reasons, as discussed in Chapter 2, *Online Identity and Personas*. From a social media context, consistency is key. If you are on multiple platforms, your peers and followers need to be able to find you and be sure it is indeed you. Using the same profile picture on each platform will help identify you.

Your profile may be considered by others outside of your friends and peer groups, so think about the images you present in your profile and what images you store. Because of the public and permanent nature of social media platforms, it is important to consider whether they reflect well on you, or if a potential employer, research sponsor or a family member might be put off, shocked, offended or disappointed by what they see.

Your image is interpreted by your readers not just from imagery, but also from the tone, content and structure of your postings. So be consistent across your platforms, with a suitable eye on why you are involved in and reading posts on each system to avoid going down rabbit holes or being plagued with notifications that take up too much of your time.

Fake news, old news, not news and the rumour mill

You will, no doubt, have been exposed to newsprint tabloid headlines. Potentially all of these will have been valid sources of news checked by an editorial team before publication. However, when reading something on social media, it is not always clear whether it has value, validity, truth and accuracy. That means that you will need to find a way of determining the difference between news, fake news, old news etc.

In social media, the postings are made by accounts often attributed to authentic news sources or respected individuals, but you should consider the social media handles presented with some caution. The Twitter handle for the publisher The Open University Press is @OpenUniPress, but without drilling deeper into the identity presented would you assume that postings by @OUP represented the publisher? Logically, most people would make that assumption, but it is always a good idea to check.

Checklist for verifying postings and ensuring validity

1 Consider the name and posting addresses. Are they as you expect? For example: Apollo 11 astronaut Buzz Aldrin's Twitter presence is @TheRealBuzz. But @buzz_aldrin_ is a privately-operated account that has nothing to do with the astronaut.

2 Is the posting the same as when it was put by the original poster or shared/retweeted? If so, how many times has it been shared or re-shared since the original posting? Has it been modified or summarised? The piece may be reported and forwarded several times from the original posting, meaning that it is not possible to see what the original source was. While an article, news piece or information source may appear in your newsfeed, it may not appear in your search results as an original piece or source.

3   Is the posting timely? Is it an old posting? This does not necessarily mean that it is no longer valid, but sometimes the material is time sensitive and so has expired in terms of interest and currency. Look closely to see if an article is in fact a reposting of something that happened previously. Often these old news postings have provocative and controversial headlines, but they are reposted to emphasise a different point.
4   Research the person or institution that posted it. Are they a bona fide expert in their field? Check the identity of the poster before accepting what they have posted as true and accurate. One of the risks of online postings through social media is that anyone can post, comment upon and repost material.
5   Is the material genuine? Material spread across the internet and stored in social media may be presented in a certain style to appear authentic. For instance, medical information about the benefits of a particular product may look as if a prestigious pharmaceutical company has developed it. Look closely at the provenance of the material before deciding on its authenticity. Has it got valid credentials such as contact details for the authors? If it appears to be corporate or product based, is it directly from the manufacturer? Is the manufacturer traceable and real?
6   Is it rumour or misinformation? When you participate in groups with your peers for support or to get course information, for instance, you might see postings that are well meant but may not be entirely accurate. Much of what you need to know will be provided by your institution in your module handbook and the course profile on your VLE. If you are unsure about anything, there is no substitute for contacting your tutor and asking just to be sure.
7   Is it valid? Validity is subjective and can only be determined by the post's relevance to whatever you are researching or reading about. Once an article or posting's provenance has been established, the material itself can be assessed and used or discarded as appropriate.

Choosing the right platform(s) to have your say

Each platform has features designed to alert you to new postings, trending posts and private/direct messages (PM/DM). While it is good to keep up to date with what is happening within your discipline on social media, creating accounts on too many different systems or subscribing to too many groups may end up with you being overloaded with information, alerts and messages. This may also use up too much of your time. It is better to gauge the value of a social media platform in terms of what it adds to your learning.

Another element to consider is what platforms and services your fellow students and tutors are using (if any). There may be an opportunity for you to drive this forward and form a group if there is nothing already in place.

> **Activity 9.3**
>
> When you have an idea of which platform you are going to use, consider the following checklist:
>
> | | Y/N |
> |---|---|
> | Does it work on all the devices you are going to use? e.g. smartphone, tablet, laptop, Mac | |
> | Can you post everything you need to on this system? e.g. text, video, graphics, photos, web links | |
> | Do you get useful information, including the information's provenance? e.g. fake news, advertising, special interest group bias | |
> | Does reading and interacting with social media expand and improve your knowledge of your subject? | |

Netiquette – speaking the language of social media

Communication between humans is largely visual, which is why photo sharing services such as Instagram, Snapchat and Tumblr are popular, despite the risk of advertising, social influencing and irrelevance. We also pick up on nuances of body language, we hear and consider the tone, force and style of delivery, and finally the interpretation of the words spoken.

In internet communications, especially social media, you tend to only get the words without any indication of how the person sending these words means them to be interpreted. As a way of giving at least some guidance from the sender to clarify the meaning of what they are saying, and for brevity, a kind of internet slang has emerged. This is similar to the form of slang used with text messaging and is also often used in spoken communication.

As well as our vocabulary changing to reflect new internet concepts and ideas, the use of language and the way that we say things online has a set of rules called netiquette (see Chapter 2, *Online Identity and Personas*, for more on this).

There is no distinct dictionary, although internet terms and phrases are now starting to appear in the Oxford English Dictionary for example: '*Vlog – A blog composed of posts in video form; (also) a video forming part of such a blog*'. Nor is there a formal set of rules explaining the usage of these terms.

A suitable example is in the abbreviation 'LOL', which is widely accepted to mean 'Laugh Out Loud', although it has been used by some with the addition of a couple of 'X' kisses to mean 'Lots of Love' XX. Because of things like this, there can be confusion and, in some cases, unintentional offence caused either to you or by you. Misunderstanding a term can radically alter the meaning of a message.

How you write your messages matters too. As with normal written English, a good grasp of grammar is important. A missing or poorly placed comma may change the sense of a sentence, as will the transposition of your and you're, or there, their and they're. Not everyone will follow the rules of grammar and sometimes it is a struggle to understand the meaning of a post.

Sometimes arguments, often referred to as *flaming*, break out regarding the poor grammar, descending into insult trading which is called a *flame war*. Think about whether you are typing in lower or upper case. Look at the two identical phrases below presented in different cases.

No, I don't need any help.
NO, I DON'T NEED ANY HELP

The first is a normal response to a question, punctuated correctly, and while it might be a little curt, it probably would not provoke much of a response. The second, all in capitals, comes across as an aggressive response. The use of capitals means that you are shouting and the message may well provoke a negative response far worse than if you were shouting at someone in real life. This is because it is much easier to express anger in writing than when physically present with someone.

Within your institution, there will be guidance on using internet services and what is expected under their own rules of netiquette. Most likely these guidance notes will be included in your course materials and posted in the institution's Visual Learning Environment and/or your Student Home Page. Following this not only within the formal sites provided by your institution but also in your personal social media is a good idea.

Some generic rules for posting and responding are:

1. Think before you post. Consider whether anything you write, or picture you post, could potentially cause any harm or embarrassment to you, or anyone else, either now or in the future. Try to avoid ambiguity and sarcasm. Angry, shouting posts do not reflect well on you and are unlikely to provoke the response you were hoping for.
2. Consider your sources. Is what you are posting honest, true and correct? If you have obtained it from an alternative source, have they properly referenced it or made certain that their posting is true, honest and correct? See 'Fake News' below.
3. When in conversation, respect the opinions of others, even if you think they are wrong. By all means engage in debate but slanging matches and belittling others usually ends up in a *flame war*. Consider how that might make *you* look. Will the posting be harmful to you? Respectfully disagreeing with an evidential discussion is what academic discourse is all about, but the emphasis is on *respectful*.

4 Unless you are writing your own blog, keep your postings brief and stick to the topic in question. Not many long rambling postings get read all the way through. If you deviate from the topic under discussion, unless your target audience is particularly interested in the tangent, you will lose their attention. Short irrelevant posts are just as likely to annoy – 'me too', for instance. Staying at around five lines or less is ideal.
5 If you do not understand what someone has posted, rather than guessing at it, respectfully ask for clarification. If the conversation thread is a long one, try and read as much of it as you can before joining in. That way, there is less likelihood of you misunderstanding the topic, repeating part of the discussion, or missing the way the debate is going.
6 Post (speak) in the same way that you would like people to speak to you.

Other tools in your posting arsenal are emoticons. Emoticons (emotion icons) are little symbols to emphasise the mood and tone of your posting, and in conversation can replace a written response. These are useful for more informal or friendly discussions such as those within your own tutor group forum or on social media. But be wary of their use in academic debate as they are not formal words and do not look professional.

Consider this example posting:

Initial post: *Fancy a coffee?*
Answer/Reply: ☺

The response with a smiley face is quite clearly in the affirmative, but there are others that can express the whole spectrum of emotion to a lesser or greater degree. Choose your emoticons wisely to ensure you get your message across in the way that you intended to. The risk with the myriad of emoticons available, particularly when using mobile social media platforms, is that the recipient may not understand the subtleties of the extensive emoticon vocabulary.

Abbreviations are regularly used and can be even more of a minefield if you do not know what they mean. The following list shows some of the more commonly used abbreviations. However, it is by no means fully inclusive of all the terms used on the internet or in texts.

Abbreviation	**Usual definition**
AFAIK	As Far As I Know
BRB	Be Right Back
CU/CU L8R	See You Later
FAQ	Frequently Asked Questions
FB	Facebook
IDC	I Don't Care
IDK	I Don't Know

IIRC	If I Recall/Remember Correctly
IMHO	In My Humble Opinion
LOL/LOLZ	Laughing Out Loud
N00B	Newbie or new user to the system
OMG	Oh My God!
OP	Original Poster
PLZ	Please
PM/DM	Personal Message (Facebook) or Direct Message (Twitter)
THX/TNX	Thanks
W00T!	Hooray!
WOOT	Want One Of Those

To avoid confusion or misunderstanding, be certain that you understand what any abbreviations mean before using them.

Evaluating your social media in the context of your Personal Learning Network

You have already considered the issue of which platform(s) are suitable for your use in previous activities, but it is important to consider how useful each platform is within your own Personal Learning Environment. Does the platform fundamentally inform your learning? It is worth thinking about a few concepts before deciding this.

Activity 9.4	Y?N
Does the platform allow you to:	
research and glean meaningful, truthful and accurate information within your discipline?	
contact your peers as needed for collaborative work, and to offer and receive support?	
interact with your tutors as needed?	
grow your internet horizons, increasing the breadth of your ability to research?	

Summary

Social media can be a useful tool to enhance and expand your learning. Used with care, you can connect with others in the same tutor group and learning community as well as with experts working within the same discipline. The primary benefits of each key platform have been discussed and you will be in a position to decide which of the platforms are most useful to you and your learning experience.

The main pitfalls of using social media have been defined along with simple strategies for avoiding these issues. This will help to keep your social media usage safer and make it a more rewarding experience.

Key points from this chapter

- Understand the key features of the major systems in social media.
- Connect with peers and tutors on these systems.
- Communicate safely and effectively in social media.
- Choose the system that matches your style of learning and your research needs.

10 Troubleshooting, Staying Safe Online

This chapter shows you:

- what to do if you run into technical problems while studying online
- how to prevent problems occurring in the first place by taking simple precautions and adopting safe online working practices.

The internet, while a useful mechanism which allows you to access and share information, is by no means a completely secure space.

How am I connected to the internet?

Your computer is connected to the internet either by Wi-Fi or an ethernet cable through to a local hub which then connects on to the internet. Your local hub is connected through to the internet by your service provider, typically a telecom or a utilities company. Sometimes, in shared accommodation, you share your internet connection with other people that live in the building.

Alternatively, you may be connected to the internet via your device's mobile data or Wi-Fi to a public access network. Most public access networks such as free Wi-Fi in libraries, internet cafés, shopping centres, restaurants or cloud services are not particularly secure. All you usually need to get access is to provide an email address.

It would be safest to not use unsecured networks or unknown services as you have no real idea what is going on behind the scenes and how much of a target for fraudsters or hackers the site might be. If there is a closed padlock symbol next to the Wi-Fi details on your screen, then the network is secured. If this is not there, it is better not to connect.

How do I know what I am connected to?

Computers and devices usually have a small indicator on their screens that show how you are connected. This is the dot and three bands of the universal Wi-Fi symbol. Often you can click or tap on it and the Wi-Fi network you are connected to will be displayed. The names are usually associated with the locale, for instance most restaurants, fast food places and coffee shops have their own name as part of the network's name.

This is called the 'SSID'. Other public access networks and city-wide Wi-Fi also tend to use their names in the SSID, and when you are at home, the SSID is usually printed on a sticker or a removable piece of plastic attached to your hub, so you will be able to see if the network you are connected to is yours or not.

> **Activity 10.1**
>
> Take a look at your broadband router in your home. Find the sticker or plastic panel that shows the Wi-Fi SSID. Take a look at the Wi-Fi connection on your device. Typically you click on the symbol for Wi-Fi on a computer and it should show you the SSID and the strength of connection measured in bars. If you are using a phone or a tablet you will need to go into your control panel and select Wi-Fi for this information.
>
> Do the SSIDs match? Is there a closed padlock next to the name? This will indicate that the network is secured by a password. You will probably see other networks listed which may be those of your neighbours and these will more than likely be secured by their own password.
>
> When you are out and about, try this again to see what services are listed. This will show what you are connected to and whether or not it is a secured network. Unsecured networks will show an open padlock symbol, or no symbol at all. Using an unsecured network makes you vulnerable to hackers and computer viruses which may compromise the security of your personal data, not to mention your academic work.

What if it says it is 'unsecured'?

This usually means that the Wi-Fi you are connected to is not protected by encryption. Encryption is where the Wi-Fi data passing to and from your device is scrambled with a secret code, making it difficult for anyone trying to 'listen in' on what you are doing on the internet. A secured network usually requires a passcode to connect to the network. On connecting, most Wi-Fi services (usually called hot spots) will ask you for a passcode. This allows you to connect to the network in a safe, encrypted way.

Is that all I need to do?

Making sure that your connection is safe is just the first step but sometimes the only connection you have is unsecured, so your internet devices need protection too. Your device is connected via mobile data, Wi-Fi or an ethernet cable through a hub or router and then on to the internet.

The internet traffic is two-way and data flows in both directions. This means that without further protection, you cannot be 100% certain that there is not a problem with some of the data you are receiving via the World Wide Web, email, messaging or through your apps.

What do I need to look out for?

There is a whole family of bad software on the internet called malware, viruses or Trojans. There are also other forms of malware that can be passed via email, messenger or social media postings which can be embedded in movie files and picture files. Malware can alter, damage or even destroy your data, and it can use your computer to attack other people's data too by stealing their email addresses or by embedding itself into files that you send.

What is a computer virus?

Computer viruses are little programs that attach themselves to computer files with the purpose of spreading themselves from computer to computer. Often these viruses have a malevolent purpose in that once spread they damage or destroy data, sometimes irrevocably. Viruses can be spread in many ways, such as by email, messaging services, the World Wide Web and by social media. Some viruses, once activated, spread themselves using your computer as a jumping off point.

What is a Trojan?

A Trojan is a program that looks like one thing but does something else. You may find them hidden on web pages looking like seemingly safe pictures or videos to download, or you may receive a message or email containing one that appears to come from someone you know. Trojans usually play on a person's curiosity to click on and run them, which is why they appear to look like something you would be interested in.

A suitable example would be an email from someone with a video attached to it. The email might use an enticing phrase like 'Check out this crazy video! It's amazing!' and an enticing name for the video like 'Crazy Cat Dance'. But the video file is not just an amusing clip, it is a is a program that deletes your data files when you click on it. The simplest approach is to never click on anything sent to you by someone that you do not know, you do not know anything about, or do not trust.

What can I do to protect my device?

The safest way to prevent malware damaging your system and data is to install security software, both anti-virus software and a firewall. These, when kept up to date, will help prevent the majority of malware from affecting your device and data.

What is anti-virus software?

This is software that will run on your device and which acts like a watchdog. It watches the data you receive and checks it for viruses and other malware threats. It works by having a database of known viruses and other malware, with each record showing the unique 'fingerprint' of a specific threat. The watchdog looks for any of these 'fingerprints' appearing in any of the files or data you access or store, and if it finds anything, it tells you right away after isolating the threat and stopping it from damaging your data.

How do I use anti-virus software?

Mostly, once it is installed you will not have to do much at all. The software runs automatically on your computer and monitors your system for threats and acts when it finds them. The only time you would need to intervene is when the software requires something like an update. Otherwise, it just sits in the background and does its job.

What is a firewall?

A computer firewall is a piece of security software that prevents unauthorised access to your computer. It works by allowing the kinds of data traffic it knows about to come into your computer and blocks everything else that it does not know about. Imagine a locked door to your house. The door lets air through, but not people, unless you open the door and let them in.

You can configure your firewall to allow certain programs to use the network connection without you having to intervene in much the same way as you would fit your door with a cat flap to let the cat come in and out at will without you having to open it. The only question you must ask yourself is do you trust the 'cat' or will you come home and find your house invaded by other creatures, all of whom can fit through your cat flap?

Where do I get anti-virus software and a firewall?

Some operating systems come with in-built protection but there are many other types of systems available as well. There are some well-established security software brands such as AVG, McAfee, Norton and Kaspersky, to name but a few, that often have their software provided free with a one-year licence when you buy a new computer. There are some free products available, normally from vendors who have a chargeable premium version with extra features.

If you are not sure how to install programs like this, do not hesitate to ask for help as it is such an important part of using the internet for study, or indeed for anything else. Your course provider is almost certain to have a Computing Help Desk, details of which will be available on your Student Home Page or by asking the Student Support Team. You could also ask for help from a local library that provides IT facilities. If you do not know which product to purchase, ask for a recommendation from someone you trust or from one of the sources of help listed above.

Once you have installed effective anti-virus and firewall software, you may find that your computer starts a little more slowly and runs a little less rapidly than without it. This is because the software is looking at everything properly and is protecting you.

Does my software need upgrading or updating?

The operating system that your computer runs will only need upgrading if a newer operating system is released. Otherwise, it may only require periodic updating, which means that patches and security fixes to remove faults, problems and bugs need to be applied from time to time. The provider will usually notify you when these things need doing and it will guide you through the process.

How do I update my computer?

The most commonly used operating systems and applications tend to have programs built into them to update their software. These updates are configured to download and apply patches and fixes automatically. You may find when you come to shut down your computer that it says something like 'Apply Updates and Shutdown?', or on starting your computer it may tell you it is applying updates. It is vitally important that you do not turn the computer off while the updates are being applied as you may damage your computer's operating system which would cause problems when you go to restart it.

Activity 10.2

Update your computer.

Check that you have the latest patches installed. With Windows you will have a program listed called 'Windows Update' which you can access through your control panel. If you have a Mac, click on the apple symbol on the top left of the screen and choose 'software update'. If there are no new updates to apply, then you are up to date. Otherwise, apply the updates suggested.

I think I have a virus, what do I do?

In all likelihood, your anti-virus software will have stopped any viruses trying to run on your system. Anti-virus software is not, however, infallible, and sometimes things do slip through the net, particularly if they are very new viruses that have not been seen before. If your device suddenly starts running a lot slower than before or behaving strangely, then it may have contracted a virus.

If you are concerned, your anti-virus software will have a facility to scan your computer to find anything that may have sneaked past your defences. Most have a deep scan feature which is a much longer process than a basic scan but well worth the effort as it leaves no stones unturned.

If your computer is completely disabled by a virus, you will need to seek professional help either through your institution's help desk or from a computer retailer. Always be sure to check the credentials of individuals offering this kind of service as they may steal your personal data or install some kind of tracking device in the process of getting your computer back up and running.

I have sent some email, but I think it may not have arrived, what should I do?

There are three main reasons why your email may not have arrived at its destination. The first is that there is a problem at the receiving end. If this is the case, you will receive an error message back from the mail system you sent it to which will include a note of what the problem is. The most common ones are 'Mailbox Full' where whoever you are sending the message to has no more space left in their mailbox to receive new messages. In this case, you would need to contact the person concerned by another means such as by telephone and let them know so that they can delete some emails to make room for new ones to come in.

Secondly, you may see an error message saying that the address you sent the message to does not exist. If this happens, check the address you are mailing; typical problems are a typing error or incorrect address.

Thirdly, sometimes your messages are intercepted by a receiving mail system because it thinks your message is junk mail, or spam as it is more commonly known. This could be because you do not have a message subject, or you have lots of internet links in it, or it contains photos or videos.

Try sending a simpler message with a filled-out subject field, and if you can, inform the recipient via an alternative method asking them to put your email address in their address book so that their computer recognises you. This should override the junk filter.

What is spam?

Think about the unsolicited paper-based junk mail that drops through your letterbox. Flyers for pizza and kebabs, letters from various companies telling you that you have won a prize, adverts for double glazing companies and cab firms, not forgetting the charity bags and appeals for money. If you have an email account, you will probably receive the electronic equivalent of this junk mail. In the IT world it is called 'spam', with the act of sending unsolicited email called 'spamming'.

You are likely to be 'spammed' if you have ever used your email address to register with an online service that has not been as careful with its data as it should. Other sources are if your email address is published on a website or social media. Spammers 'harvest' email addresses from these sites and services and compile lists of addresses which they then spam with their messages. Additionally, if you have ever received some spam and responded to it, the sender will have been able to confirm that the address they sent the message to exists and is active.

What does spam look like?

Spam mail tends to follow a fairly similar pattern. Firstly, it is likely to offer a service or a warning about something you do not normally engage with or buy. But the content may be of a darker nature involving enticing you to access a pornographic site, or purchase 'adult' goods and services.

Sometimes the mail can have a financial nature suggesting investments or sending money to the needy, usually with a substantial return to yourself to sweeten the pot. Spam mail can be infected with computer viruses and can be 'armed' with a Trojan program. Spam can also be designed to steal your information through 'phishing'.

If, however, you are happy to receive emails from particular retailers or companies, you can add their email address to your email address book and then they will automatically go into your inbox.

What can I do about spam?

Most email services and programs have an element of filtering built into them. Mainstream email services such as Gmail automatically divert any mail sent to you that they are aware is spam into a junk mail folder that you can see in your email program. Also, they have smart filters and scanners that consider each piece of email that comes in via their system and assess any potential risk.

Emails with known viruses and Trojans are usually rejected. However, some do get through but ought to be stopped by your up-to-date anti-virus software. Mail that is full of internet links (known as hyperlinks), has no subject field or has suspect content such as being filled with imagery or video files can be flagged up as spam and dropped into your junk mail folder too. This gives you the opportunity to review the content of your junk folder in case something that someone has legitimately sent you has been flagged as spam, and if so, you can transfer it back to your inbox.

If you receive a message in your inbox that looks suspicious, that you did not request or are uncertain where it came from, *do not open it*. Either drop it into your junk folder or delete it outright.

What is phishing?

Phishing is a scamming attempt to extract information from you in order to use your identity for something. This is usually in the form of a message received on your phone, by email or a messaging system trying to get you to click on a link and provide your personal information.

It will probably be camouflaged as a message from a supposedly official and trustworthy source like a bank or a company you use often, such as your internet provider, the Inland Revenue, Amazon, eBay or PayPal, usually warning you about a problem and asking you to confirm your details. They may ask for your name, date of birth, account number, passwords, etc. While they look convincing, your bank or a real company you deal with will not ask you for that information via the World Wide Web in any format.

Another giveaway is when you receive an 'urgent message' from a bank but you do not have an account with it. There are usually certain little tell-tale signs, mostly poor grammar in the text, or your name being spelled incorrectly. But in any event, if you receive such a message, and you do actually have an account with the alleged sender, it is important not to click on anything or follow any links.

Say, for example, the email says it has come from your bank, and you are not sure whether or not it is genuine, you should not respond to the email. Instead, telephone your bank using the phone number you already have and *not* the one offered in the email. You can then ask if the email is genuine and deal with anything you need to that way.

Banks will never email and ask for details of your accounts, your pin number or ask you to transfer money. If you do get an email that you suspect is fraudulent, it can be very helpful to let the bank, or company, know because it means that they can contact their other customers to warn them. The email can also be investigated by their fraud department.

Other types of phishing might come from companies that you do indeed use, threatening to suspend your access if you do not respond, or confirm certain personal details. These too should be ignored and, as with the bank example above, you should contact the provider of that service with a phone number or email that you *already* hold and check whether it is genuine.

With this type of phishing, the point of the exercise is to frighten you with a threat of losing a particular service, such as your internet connection, if you do not respond, almost like bait on a hook. It might look as if it comes from a particular company as it embraces the look and feel of the service and makes no particularly outrageous offers which might otherwise alert you, but it actually comes from a scammer.

How can I make sure that my password is secure?

Lots of systems such as your online banking, social media, email, etc. require a username and password to use them. The username is the name you log on to the system with, which is then validated by your password. Some systems use your email address as a username.

However, it is crucial that you do not use the same username and password combinations on all of the systems that you use. Imagine if you used the same username and password on your social media as you did for your bank. If your social media account were to be hacked into and your password revealed, they then have access to your bank account too. Not only will they be able to see your photos and harvest the details of your contacts on social media, they may also be able to steal your money.

Your passwords should be memorable to you, but not easily guessable by someone who knows a bit about you. Do not use the name of your pet, or your car registration, just as you should not use your date of birth for your ATM PIN code. Do not use short passwords as cracking programs can break them easily, and do not stick to just numbers or letters. You could also try using a piece of information that no one else knows.

The most secure passwords have a combination of upper- and lower-case letters, numbers and, where allowed, special characters like $, & and @. Have a look at the passwords below:

Password	Comments
PASSWORD	Far too easy to guess, too short and all the same case. Try not to use real words that a password breaking program can figure out.
Passw0rd	Better but still guessable and transposing just one character will not hold back a password cracker program for long.
478Monday01	Harder to guess but still with guessable elements.
W@Tt6fL09D$	Long enough, complex enough and very difficult to guess. This is an example of a good password but one that may be very difficult for you to remember.
?!060722@HerneBay!*	This is long enough and very difficult to guess but easier to remember. It might be, for example, the date of birth of a family member together with their place of birth and a combination of special characters.

Whatever you decide to use, do not write it down anywhere that it can easily be found and do not tell anyone you do not trust what it is.

How can I shop and pay online safely?

These days a sizeable proportion of essential and non-essential purchases of goods and services are made online. This book may have been bought online for instance. There are established companies with solid reputations and a track record of safety and security, but there are also numerous new and emerging sites and services appearing every day. There are a few simple checks you can make to be sure that they are safe for you to use.

Firstly, is the site secured with an SSL certificate? This means the connection between your computer and the site is secured with encryption so no one can intercept your transaction. If there is a good secure connection, you should be able to see a small padlock next to the address of the site in the address bar of your web browser. The little padlock should be clickable, which will then show you the details about the certificate that guarantees that your connection is properly secured.

Payment methods are also indicative of the security of the site. If the site uses PayPal, the PayPal address should be clearly stated and correlate with the address of the site or service. For instance, if you are buying event tickets from a ticket site called 'TicketMeNow' but the purchase address is 'Joe.Bloggs@mail.com', it is likely that there is something awry. Before sending any money, make sure that you have verified, as far as you possibly can, that the site is real, and the service or product that you are purchasing is real.

Purchasing via PayPal gives you some online protection in that you can look up the address you are sending payment to and see if their contact details have been verified. Additionally, there is a mechanism for querying transactions if there is a problem, with the aim of getting your money back.

Only ever use protected payments. For instance, your credit card will give you some purchase protection that you may not have using a debit card or other forms of payment. Check with your card provider for details. Unless you are 100% certain of your seller, *never* pay by bank transfer as you will not get your money back if there is a problem.

I think I passed on some personal information, what should I do?

First things first: change all your passwords, especially to your online banking and any vital system that you use. If you think that credit/debit card or bank details have been compromised, tell your card provider and/or bank immediately.

They have procedures to help protect you from fraud and are contactable 24 hours a day by telephone or banking app. If you cannot find the direct numbers for your bank or credit card's fraud department, use the one on the back of your credit/debit card and ask to be put through.

> **Activity 10.3**
>
> Think about your personal information that you keep on your computer and routinely use. How much of it are you happy for other people to see? How much can you do without? What is absolutely vital to you and what have you done to make sure it is safe?
>
> Change your passwords!

And finally …

Trust your instincts. If something looks too good to be true, then it probably is too good to be true! If something does not *look* right, it probably is *not* right! Most internet scams give themselves away by being too greedy, constructed with poor grammar and/or spelling, and are poorly targeted, but this is by no means the case with all of them. Some are very convincing, so be aware, exercise common sense and trust your instincts.

There may have been other people who have been taken in by the scam, and you may be able to find out about this by carrying out a simple internet search. The general rule is: if you are unsure about anything, *do not do it!*

Summary

When you are using online resources and participating in online study there are risks, and while they may be very slight, they can threaten your data, your identity and your ongoing study. Cyber security needs to be taken seriously. When you carry out online research, if the site you are looking at contains lots of adverts, it is best to click away and find something else.

When you are shopping and paying online, ensure that you can see the closed padlock symbol on your web browser showing that your connection is properly secured. This way you can satisfy yourself that the site you are on is reputable and real, and that your purchases and transactions are safe. If you keep hold of your personal information on your computer, keep your passwords different, complex and hard to guess, and protect your computer with suitable security software, then you should not have a problem.

Key points from this chapter

- Computer security is important.
- Safe practice online prevents problems.
- Update your computer regularly.
- Install suitable security software such as anti-virus and firewall solutions.
- Backup your data.
- Change your passwords.
- Think before you click.

Bibliography

American Numismatic Society, 2022. [Online] Available at: https://numismatics.org
Ancient Origins, 2022. [Online] Available at: www.ancient-origins.net
Ariadne, 2021. *The SISinHE Centre: Web CT Accessibility*. [Online] Available at: http://www.ariadne.ac.uk/issue/23/disinhe/
Ashe, S. J. & Lopez, R. M., 2020. Communication in online learning – how important is it?. *The Clearing House*, Volume 94 (1), pp. 15–30.
Auris, 2021. *Hearing Loop Systems*. [Online] Available at: http://aurisloops.com/
Avast, 2021. *What is Trojan Malware?*. [Online] Available at: https://www.avast.com/c-trojan#gref
AVG, 2021. *AVG AntiVirus*. [Online] Available at: https://www.avg.com
Babbel, 2021. *Learn a language*. [Online] Available at: https://www.babbel.com/
Balabolka, 2021. [Online] Available at: https://balabolka.en.softonic.com/
BBC News, 2022. [Online] Available at: https://www.bbc.co.uk
Big White Wall, 2021. [Online] Available at: www.bigwhitewall.com
Blackboard, 2021. *Blackboard Learn Help for Students*. [Online] Available at: https://help.blackboard.com/Learn/Student
Cambridge English Dictionary, 2022. [Online] Available at: https://dictionary.cambridge.org/dictionary/english
Canvas, 2021. *Instructure*. [Online] Available at: https://www.instructure.com/en-gb/canvas
Capti Voice, 2021. [Online] Available at: https://www.captivoice.com/capti-site//
Cela, K., Sicilia, M.-Á. & Sánchez-Alonso, S., 2016. Influence of learning styles on social structures in online learning environments. *British Journal of Educational Technology*, Volume 47 (6), pp. 1065–1082.
Cole, A. W., Lennon, L. & Weber, N. L., 2021. Student perceptions of online active learning practices and online learning climate predict online course engagement. *Interactive Learning Environments*, Volume 29 (5), pp. 866–880.
DataReportal, 2021. *Global Social Media Stats*. [Online] Available at: https://datareportal.com/social-media-users
Diigo, 2021. *Your Learning Simplified*. [Online] Available at: https://www.diigo.com/
Disabled Student Allowance, 2021. *Help if you're a student with a learning difficulty, health problem or disability*. [Online] Available at: https://www.gov.uk/disabled-students-allowance-dsa
Dragon, 2021. *Dragon Anywhere: Dictate Now*. [Online] Available at: https://apps.apple.com/us/app/dragon-anywhere-dictate-now
Dropbox, 2021. *Store, share, collaborate and more with Dropbox*. [Online] Available at: https://www.dropbox.com/
Duolingo, 2021. *The World's Best Way to Learn a Language*. [Online] Available at: https://www.duolingo.com/
EduApps, 2021. [Online] Available at: http://eduapps.org
Evernote, 2021. *Tame your work, organize your life*. [Online] Available at: https://evernote.com/
Facebook, 2021. [Online] Available at: https://en-gb.facebook.com/

Facebook, 2021. *Terms of Service*. [Online] Available at: https://en-gb.facebook.com/legal/terms

Flaticon, 2021. *UK Icons*. [Online] Available at: https://www.flaticon.com/free-icons/uk

Frith, L., May, G. & Pocklington, A., 2017. *A Student's Guide to Online Mentoring*. London: Palgrave Macmillan.

GDPR, 2021. *General Data Protection Regulation*. [Online] Available at: https://gdpr-info.eu/

Gibbs, G., 1988. *Learning by Doing: A Guide to Teaching and Learning Methods*. London: Further Education Unit.

Glasby, A., 2021. *Visual Stress*. [Online] Available at: http://www.anitaglasbyoptometry.co.uk/products-and-services/visual-stress/

Google, 2021. *Google Drive*. [Online] Available at: https://www.google.com/intl/en-GB/drive/download/

Google, 2021. *Speech-to-Text*. [Online] Available at: https://cloud.google.com/speech-to-text

Google Search Community, 2022. [Online] Available at: https://support.google.com/websearch/community?hl=en-GB

Health and Safety Executive, 2021. *Good posture when using display screen equipment*. [Online] Available at: https://www.hse.gov.uk/msd/dse/good-posture.htm

Heath and Safety Executive, 2021. *DES Assessments and Healthy Working*. [Online] Available at: https://www.hsl.gov.uk/dse-assessments-and-healthy-working

History from Below, 2022. [Online] Available at: https://feedly.com/i/entry/o1CRMgat-J0FX72mfdLkXqAY4l45lVmlxIVjMVLAL/8c=_178b1c4eb36:e25e:ff51788f

Hoi, V. N. & Le Hang, H., 2021. The structure of student engagement in online learning: A bi-factor exploratory structural equation modelling approach. *Journal of Computer Assisted Learning*, Volume 37 (4), pp. 1141–1153.

Huang, Q., 2019. Comparing teacher's roles of F2f learning and online learning in a blended English course. *Computer Assisted Language Learning*, Volume 32 (3), pp. 190–209.

Instagram, 2021. [Online] Available at: https://www.instagram.com

Instapaper, 2021. *Save Anything. Read Anywhere*. [Online] Available at: https://www.instapaper.com/

Kapersky, 2021. *What is a Trojan horse and what damage can it do?*. [Online] Available at: https://www.kaspersky.co.uk/resource-center/threats/trojans

Keates, A., 2017. *Dyslexia and Information and Communications Technology: A Guide for Teachers and Parents*. London: David Fulton Publishers.

Kehrwald, B., 2008. Understanding social presence in text-based online learning environments. *Distance Education*, Volume 29 (1), pp. 89–106.

Knightley, W. M., 2007. Adult learners online: Students' experiences of learning online. *Australian Journal of Adult Learning*, Volume 47 (2), pp. 264–288.

Knowles, C. B., 2021. *Comfort Classics: Classical Studies Support*. [Online] Available at: https://classicalstudies.support/home/comfort-classics/

LetMeType, 2021. [Online] Available at: https://letmetype.en.softonic.com/

Lewis, H. & Price-Howard, K., 2021. Worlds collide: Traditional classroom meets online learning. *Journal of Hospitality & Tourism Research (Washington, D.C.)*, Volume 45 (5), pp. 924–926.

Lim, J. R. N., Rosenthal, S., Sim, Y. J. M., Lim, Z.-Y. & Oh, K. R., 2021. Making online learning more satisfying: The effects of online-learning self-efficacy, social presence and content structure. *Technology, Pedagogy and Education*, Volume 30 (4), pp. 543–556.

LinkedIn, 2021. *LinkedIn Etiquette, 20 Do's and Don'ts*. [Online] Available at: https://www.linkedin.com/pulse/20140417174121-34888774-linkedin-etiquette-guide-20-do-s-don-ts

McAfee, 2021. *Total Protection*. [Online] Available at: https://www.mcafee.com

Messenger, 2021. *Hang out anytime, anywhere*. [Online] Available at: https://www.messenger.com/

Microsoft, 2021. *OneDrive Personal Cloud Storage*. [Online] Available at: https://www.microsoft.com/en-ww/microsoft-365/onedrive/online-cloud-storage

Moodle, 2021. [Online] Available at: https://moodle.org/

Moore, J. L., Dickson-Deane, C. & Galyen, K., 2011. e-Learning, online learning, and distance learning environments: Are they the same?. *The Internet and Higher Education*, Volume 14 (2), pp. 129–135.

Muir, T., Milthorpe, N. & Stone, C. D., 2019. Chronicling engagement: Students' experience of online learning over time. *Distance Education*, Volume 40 (2), pp. 262–277.

My Study Bar, 2021. [Online] Available at: https://www.eduapps.org/mystudybar/

Nall, R., 2018. *Medical News Today*. [Online] Available at: https://www.medicalnewstoday.com/articles/321536

NaturalReader, 2021. *Powerful Text-to-Speech for at home, work, or on the go*. [Online] Available at: https://www.naturalreaders.com/

NHS, 2021. *How to sit at your desk correctly*. [Online] Available at: https://www.nhs.uk/live-well/healthy-body/how-to-sit-correctly/

Nightline, 2021. [Online] Available at: www.nightline.org.uk

Norton, 2021. [Online] Available at: https://uk.norton.com

Office for National Statistics, 2019. [Online] Available at: https://www.ons.gov.uk

OpenAthens, 2021. *My Athens*. [Online] Available at: https://my.openathens.net/

Oxford English Dictionary, 2021. [Online] Available at: https://www.oed.com/

Phishing, 2021. *What is Phishing?*. [Online] Available at: https://www.phishing.org/what-is-phishing

Questionmark, 2021. *Online assessment tools*. [Online] Available at: https://www.questionmark.com

Quora, 2022. [Online] Available at: https://www.quora.com/

Reddit, 2022. [Online] Available at: https://www.reddit.com

Rosetta Stone, 2021. *Speak a New Language with Confidence*. [Online] Available at: https://www.rosettastone.co.uk

Saxons, 2021. *5 Information Security Threats SMEs Could Be Facing*. [Online] Available at: https://www.saxonsit.com.au/blog/tech/5-information-security-threats-smes-facing/

Schaefer, T., Fabian, C. M. & Kopp, T., 2020. The dynamics of online learning at the workplace: Peer-facilitated social learning and the application in practice. *British Journal of Educational Technology*, Volume 51 (4), pp. 1406–1419.

Science Museum, 2022. [Online] Available at: https://www.sciencemuseum.org.uk

Skype, 2021. [Online] Available at: https://www.skype.com/en/

Snapchat, 2021. [Online] Available at: https://www.snapchat.com/

Spencer, S., 2021. *Google Power Search*. [Online] Available at: https://www.oreilly.com/library/view/google-power-search/9781449311940/ch01.html

Statistica, 2021. *Twitter – Statistics & Facts*. [Online] Available at: https://www.statista.com/topics/737/twitter/

Student Minds, 2021. [Online] Available at: www.studentminds.org.uk

The American Folk Song Collection, 2022. [Online] Available at: https://kodaly.hnu.edu

The Conversation, 2021. [Online] Available at: https://theconversation.com/uk/topics/classics-618

The Daily Telegraph, 2022. [Online] Available at: https://www.telegraph.co.uk

Tik Tok, 2021. [Online] Available at: https://www.tiktok.com/en/

Twitter, 2021. *Happening Now*. [Online] Available at: https://twitter.com/?lang=en

University of Kent, 2021. *Assignment Survival Kit*. [Online] Available at: https://www.kent.ac.uk/ai/ask/index.php

Wenger, E., 1998. *Communities of Practice: Learning, Meaning and Identity*. New York: Cambridge University Press.

WhatsApp, 2021. *Simple. Secure. Reliable Messaging*. [Online] Available at: https://www.whatsapp.com/

Wiki Answers, 2022. [Online] Available at: https://www.wiki.answers.com

Wikitravel, 2022. [Online] Available at: https://wikitravel.org/en/Main_Page

WordTalk, 2021. [Online] Available at: https://www.wordtalk.org.uk/

XMind, 2021. [Online] Available at: https://www.xmind.net/

YouTube, 2021. [Online] Available at: https://www.youtube.com/

Zembylas, M., 2008. Adult learners' emotions in online learning. *Distance Education*, Volume 29 (1), pp. 71–87.

Zephoria, 2021. *The Top 10 Valuable Facebook Statistics – Q2 2021*. [Online] Available at: https://zephoria.com/top-15-valuable-facebook-statistics/

Zoom, 2021. [Online] Available at: https://zoom.us/

Appendix 1

Activity 2.8 suggested answers

Below is an example of academic voice. Try rewriting the other two phrases using an academic voice.

Example 1

Day-to-day voice: Thanks for that. I was going to have a bit of a rummage later and try and find out where it is. Any clue where the homework is?

Academic voice: Many thanks. I will have a look later to see if I can find it. Do you know how to access the assignments?

Example 2

Day-to-day voice: Not only is Elizabeth 1 the largest aspect of the painting, even out of proportion to the surrounding characters and furniture, this portrayal of her really signifies how she is a larger than life character to look up to and makes her this focal point both within this painting but also within Elizabethan society.

Academic voice: Elizabeth is the focus of the painting, and the surrounding characters and furniture are out of proportion.

Example 3

Day-to-day voice: The translation of this letter by Cicero isn't that clear – in the translation he's actually mentioned as one of the speakers, writing was what he did for a living, so it is important to him for the speaker – to be known. But in this translation, we don't know if he is the actual speaker or not.

Academic voice: Cicero was a writer and because he is mentioned as such in this text, it is unclear whether he is writing in his own voice or that of a persona.

Appendix 2

Activity 5.4: Identifying your learning style and strengths

If you had mostly a's, then your strength is learning visually. Perhaps you:

- Sketch course content. Even the simplest sketch can help you remember ideas.
- List your tasks – even the ones you have completed – just to have the satisfaction of visually crossing out tasks done.
- Write notes on your favourite coloured sticky-notes to help you remember and paste them around.
- Find that an uncluttered desk helps to clear your mind, which in turn helps you study better.
- Write yourself encouraging notes and post them where you can see them.
- Create mind maps, flowcharts or other graphic organisers.

If you had mostly b's, then your strength is auditory, learning by listening. Perhaps you:

- Listen to the recordings of tutorials for reference and repetition. It might also help if you listen to things at the same time as other things or before falling asleep.
- Read your textbook and notes out loud as you study. You could even record them as you do so.
- Teach yourself to read aloud in your mind without making sound. During exams, you will be able hear the questions as well as see them.
- Set up an online study group and arrange to meet in an online platform such as Skype, Facebook or Zoom. When studying with others, you can hear what they say, and hear yourself teaching them as well. This will reinforce your understanding of the material.
- Proofread your assignments by reading them aloud.

If you had mostly c's, then your strength is kinaesthetic, learning by doing. Perhaps you:

- Take notes creatively. For instance, drawing quick pictures in class that relate to the material being taught.
- Ask and answer questions before, during and after class.
- Make models of the concepts whenever possible.

- If possible, move around while you are studying.
- Draw flowcharts, mind maps or simply rewrite the notes.
- Incorporate pictures of models, if possible.
- Make physical comfort a priority as you study.
- Make note cards and create sample tests that you can take for review.

Appendix 3

Getting support and funding

The Disabled Students' Allowance (DSA) is a government scheme which provides financial help to students to cover some of the extra costs they have because of a mental health problem, long-term illness or any other disability. The first thing you should do is check with your university or college that your course is recognised as one of the following:

- a first degree, e.g. BA, BSc or BEd
- Foundation Degree
- Certificate of Higher Education
- Diploma of Higher Education (DipHE)
- Higher National Certificate (HNC)
- Higher National Diploma (HND)
- Postgraduate Certificate of Education (PGCE)
- a postgraduate course
- initial teacher training.

For part-time students, your course intensity can affect how much you get. 'Course intensity' means how long your course takes to complete each year compared to an equivalent full-time course. You can check course intensity with your university or college. The rules are different depending on your course.

Most course providers will help you with making an application and will be able to advise you on the kind of additional support that they can offer you. DSA is not means-tested so long as you meet the criteria.

You can apply for DSA if you live in England and have a disability that affects your ability to study such as:

- a learning difficulty, e.g. dyslexia or ADHD
- a mental health condition such as anxiety or depression
- a physical disability, e.g. you are partially sighted or have to use crutches
- a long-term health condition such as cancer, chronic heart disease or HIV.

You must also:

- be an undergraduate or postgraduate student (including Open University or distance learning)
- qualify for student finance from Student Finance England and be studying on a course that lasts at least a year.

You cannot get DSA from Student Finance England if you are:

- an EU student
- eligible for the NHS Disabled Students' Allowance (this is a separate scheme)
- getting equivalent support from another funding source, such as from your university or a social work bursary.

It does not matter what other money you or other members of your household have coming in. You will receive any DSA on top of your other student finance and you will not have to repay it. You can apply for this funding through the gov.uk website.

DSA can be used to pay for:

- specialist equipment, e.g. a computer if you need one because of your disability
- non-medical helpers
- extra travel because of your disability
- other disability-related costs of studying.

You may be able to get a new computer if you do not already have one, or your current one does not meet your study needs. More information will be provided to you if you are assessed as needing a new computer.

It cannot be stressed too highly how useful the assistive technology is. DSA pays for training to use the software that you are given and it is advisable to take advantage of this so that you get the best from the programs and equipment. There are also training videos that come with the software and additional information on the manufacturers' websites. For more details about DSA in higher education, go to https://www.gov.uk/disabled-students-allowance-dsa. Even if you do not qualify for DSA, it is still important to tell your course provider if there is anything that is likely to have an impact on your ability to study. There is every possibility that they can help with whatever it is!

Applying for DSA

To show that you qualify for DSA, you will need to provide evidence that you have an incapacity, medical condition, sensory impairment, physical disability, mental health condition, or a specific learning difficulty (such as dyslexia) that affects your ability to study. This evidence will need to be sent together with any application to the appropriate funding provider.

You will need to provide proof of your eligibility by supplying a disability evidence form. This form can be downloaded from https://www.gov.uk/disabled-students-allowance-dsa and once you have filled in your details, you need to send it to your medical practitioner to complete and sign. You then send that form to the DSA for them to complete your application. You can also get extra help to pay for a new diagnostic assessment for learning difficulties which you can apply for through your college or university.

Appendix 4

Activity 7.3 answers

Consider the most common types of web pages as listed below and consider whether or not you think that they are suitable sources of information for academic work.

Type of website: Blogs. Not suitable for academic work.
Examples: Ancient Origins; History from Below
The information contained within sites like this can be very useful in informing your thinking, but they are neither academic nor peer reviewed.

Type of website: Wikis. Not suitable for academic work.
Examples: Wikipedia; Wikitravel
These are useful because they provide background information on a topic, but they do not have a single identifiable author and some can be edited and amended by members of the public. Where a wiki has academic references, these should be followed up and used instead.

Type of website: Q & A sites. Not suitable for academic work.
Examples: Wiki Answers; Quora
These are useful in that they might provide general information about a topic. Any information found here should be independently verified and located in a reliable source with an identifiable author.

Type of website: Forums or groups. Not suitable for academic work.
Examples: Google Help Community; Reddit
These are useful for informing your thinking in that they allow people to give their opinions on various topics. They may also provide information or links to other sources but should not be quoted or cited as a source of information as they do not constitute a published, peer-reviewed source.

Type of website: Scholarly works. Suitable for academic work.
Examples: books.google.com; scholar.google.com; academia.edu; jstor.org
These are either electronic copies or scans of published peer-reviewed writing from academic sources. The provenance of the author(s) can be traced and verified. They also contain bibliographies which verify the sources that have been used, which add weight to the arguments contained and which are also useful for finding additional information on your chosen topic.

Type of website: News articles. Suitable for academic work.
Examples: The Daily Telegraph; BBC News

These sites contain electronic versions of news items and may be useful for some types of academic work. Caution is advised in terms of the editorial quality of the work and its intended readership. To be on the safe side, it is best to check with your course leader that a specific site is suitable for the task you are working on.

Type of website: Databases and archives. Suitable for academic work.

Examples: The American Folk Song Collection; The American Numismatic Society

Although it is not always possible to identify the individual or organisation that has compiled the database, these types of sites bring together lots of examples which can be found and followed up on elsewhere. The best quality databases will include details on how to search and cite their content.

Type of website: Documents, PDF files. Suitable for academic work.

Examples: Google Docs (documents, spreadsheets, presentations, etc.); PowerPoint presentations; Excel spreadsheets; Word documents.

Useful, but this depends on the kind of document and what it contains. These might be PDF documents, Excel spreadsheets or PowerPoints. These are documents, or scans of documents, that are uploaded by individuals or organisations. Although it is sometimes possible to identify the author, this is not always the case. Where possible, follow up on the evidence presented for yourself in other sources. To be on the safe side, check the provenance of the author and consult your tutor or course leader before using.

Type of website: Information pages. Not suitable for academic work.

Examples: Science Museum; Top Ten Most Beautiful Victorian Buildings

Sources like these contain general information but may or may not have an individual named author. They may be interesting and inform your thinking, but they are not necessarily academic in tone or peer reviewed. Sites supplied by museums and the like may be useful but this should be checked with your tutor or course leader before use.

Index

abbreviations, social media 138–9
ability/disability 72
academic identity 86–8, 90
academic voice 23–6
accessibility 3–4, 72
advantages of online study 29–30
anti-virus software 144–5, 146
assessment 60, 100
assignments, and timelines 100–3
auditory learners 76
audits, study skills 66–8
authenticity, of online sources 108–10

backing up and restoring work 114–15, 117
bibliographic details 103
blended courses 1–2, 48
blind/partially sighted 80–1
blogging 126–7
bookmarking tools 108
books, as sources 99, 103
brain (the) 34
branding, personal 93–6

calendars 39–40, 52, 100
challenges 85–6
choosing courses 2–3
collaborative learning 43
communication
　with others 7
　and social media 132–3
　with tutors 22–3, 46–8, 89, 132–3
　see also forums
confidence 54–5, 82, 85
Continuing Professional Development courses 26–7, 85–6, 88–9
course leaders *see* tutors
course material 4, 76–7
COVID pandemic 7–8

deaf /hard of hearing 81–2
digital footprints 10, 16
disability
　and accessibility 3–4, 72
　see also blind/partially sighted; deaf; learning difficulties

distance learning 1
dyslexia 77–8

educational support software 123–4
email
　communication with tutors/course leaders 22–3, 89
　effective writing 44–6
　not arriving 146
　spam 146–8
　and the Student Home Page 59
emoticons 138
employability 94–6
etiquette 17–18, 88–9
experience, of online courses 7–8

face-to-face meetings 48
Facebook 122–3, 128–9
feedback 68, 88
filing/retrieving work 115–16
firewalls 144–5
format of course material 76–7
forums 60–1
　and academic voice 23–6
　keyboard bravery/behaviour 18–21
　netiquette 17–18
　and online profiles 13
　and studying online 33, 41–3
　welcome 3, 7, 16–17

General Data Protection Regulations (GDPR) 11
generic learning outcomes 57–8
group work 48–51, 61

handbooks, course 52–3
headsets 120
health and safety 38–9
hearing, hard of 81–2
honesty 15–16
hot spots 142

identity *see* academic identity; online identity
image sharing 127–8

Index 165

independent learning 62–3
integrity 15–16
interacting 6–7, 43, 121
   and academic voice 23–6
   and the learning community 60–1
internet connection 31, 112–13, 141–3

joining in 31, 33, 60–2
journal articles 99

key words 99, 100, 102, 104, 107–8
keyboard bravery 18–21
kinaesthetic learners 76

learning community 60–2
learning difficulties 70–2, 76
   dyslexia 77–8
   speech-to-text/vice versa 79
   visual stress 78–9
   see also blind; deaf
Learning Journals 66, 68
learning outcomes 56–8
learning styles 74–6
libraries 102–4, 112

malware 143
Managed Learning Environments (MLEs) 121
Massive Open Online Courses (MOOCs) 26
mental health 73–4
mentoring, peer 63–4
microblogging 127
   see also Twitter
microphones 82, 120
MyStudyBar 72–3

National Union of Students (NUS) 59
netiquette 17–18
   and social media 136–9
   see also keyboard bravery

online identity/personas 14–15, 90, 133–4
   and the academic voice 23–6
   CPD courses 26–7
   email communication with tutors/course leaders 22–3
   honesty and integrity 15–16
   keyboard bravery 18–21
   MOOCs 26
   netiquette 17–18

online personas 14–15
online profiles 10–14
   welcome forums 16–17
online presence 15, 26, 85–6, 93
online profiles 10–14, 91–2, 93–4
operating systems 117, 145
overlays 77–8, 79

partially sighted *see* blind/partially sighted
passwords 13, 59, 114, 149–50
   compromised 150–1
payments, online 150
peers
   communication 132–3
   meeting 90–3
   mentoring 63–4
peripherals, computer 118–20
personal branding 93–6
personal information, compromised 150–1
Personal Learning Environment (PLE) 37, 112–13, 139
personas *see* online identity/personas
phishing 148–9
photographs, and online profiles 13–14, 26, 94, 134
planning 53–4, 83
   internet searches 106–8
   timelines 100–2
   visual plans 79–80
posture 38–9
presence *see* online presence
primary sources 99–100
priority boards 62–3
profiles *see* online profiles

reflection 66–70
research 98–9, 110–11
   academic sources 99–100
   and authenticity of online sources 108–10
   bookmarking tools 108
   library catalogues 102–4
   planning internet search 106–8
   search terms 104–6
   timelines 100–2
resources 60, 113–14

safeguarding work/data 117
search terms 104–6

security online
    anti-virus software/firewalls 144–5
    and email 146–9
    internet connections 141–3
    passwords 149–50
    and personal information 150–1
    shopping and paying 150
    upgrading/updating computers 145
    viruses/Trojans/ Malware 143, 146
security software 143–4
self
    academic 86–8
    and personal branding 93–6
shopping safely 150
skills, study 56–8
social media 31, 122–3
    blogging 126
    choosing platforms 135–6
    and communication 132–3
    Facebook 122–3, 128–9
    image sharing 127–8
    microblogging 127
    news validity 134–5
    online identity 133–4
    and Personal Learning Environment (PLE) 139
    Twitter 123, 129–32
    vlogging 127
sources, academic 99–100, 102–6, 108–10
space for study 34–8, 70
spam 146–8
speech-to-text/text-to-speech difficulties 79
SSIDs 142
SSL certificates 150
storage, digital 114, 117
Student Home Pages 4, 39, 43, 53, 58–62
Student Support Teams 53, 73, 77, 121
study skills 5
    audits 66–8
study space 34–8, 70
studying online 33
    and the brain 34
    and study space 34–8
styles of learning 74–6

subject-specific learning outcomes 56–7
support, peer 5–6

table magnifiers 81
team working 48–51
technologies
    assistive 72–3, 78, 79–81
    backing up and restoring 114–15, 117
    digital resources 113–14
    educational support software 123–4
    filing/retrieving work 115–16
    internet connection 112–13
    miscellaneous devices/hardware 118–20
    safeguarding work/data 117
    Virtual Learning Environments (VLEs) 120–2
    see also social media
time management 39–41, 62, 70
timelines, and research 100–2
Trojans 143, 147
tutorials 43–4
tutors
    communication with 22–3, 46–8, 89, 132–3
    getting to know 89–90
Twitter 123

unsecured Wi-Fi 142

virtual campuses 32
Virtual Learning Environments (VLEs) 120–2
viruses, computer 143, 146
visual learners 76
visual plans 79–80
visual stress 78–9
vlogging 127
vocabulary 25–6
    social media 136–9
voice, academic 23–6

Welcome Forums 3, 7, 16–17
Wi-Fi 112–13
workplace, and academic identity 86
writing, effective 44–6